BREAK UP
WAKE UP
MOVE ON

From Broken Heart to Open Heart;
Prepare for the Partner You've Always Longed For

Randy Siegel

Break Up, Wake Up, Move On
From Broken Heart to Open Heart; Prepare for the Partner You've Always Longed For

Wyngate Publishing

Printed in the United States of America

Self-Help—Relationship

ISBN: 978-0-9976418-0-6

Praise For

Break Up, Wake Up, Move On

"*Break Up, Wake Up, Move On* will help anyone who is on the tumultuous journey through the shadow side of being in a relationship—being out of one. Drawing on personal experience, conversations with friends, and literature, Randy Siegel shows us that breakups are as transformative as the relationships that precede them. He also reminds us that transformation requires the same attention and surrender that love does. Written in a tone that is kind and honest, this is a beautiful book about a difficult time."

Laura Hope-Gill

"Randy Siegel nails it again. In this epiphany-filled work, Siegel shares his own story while offering practical how-to advice to help readers mend, grow—even thrive—during one of life's more painful passages, the breakup of a relationship."

Elizabeth Bridgers

"Randy sent me his book after I told him that my relationship had ended the week before. That Saturday morning I curled up with the book and didn't get up until I'd finished it. I saw myself on every page, in every chapter, and in every emotion. There was no part that I couldn't relate to. Randy opened his soul so that readers can see what he experienced and recognize themselves. I was grateful to have this book when I needed it most, and now that several weeks have passed, I think I need to read it again!"

Susan Koscis

"It's a cliché, but it's so very true—'breaking up is hard to do.' And, worse, it can be devastating to get over. In a memoir-like style Randy Siegel reminds us that we always have options. To wallow in misery, self-loathing, doubt, fear, blame, self-pity, or loneliness after the dissolution of a relationship is clearly an option, but we have other choices. Randy invites us into his heart and head as he learns to be present with his feelings and to grasp the realities of the emotionally charged weeks and months following a breakup. As a reader you'll find yourself more than an observer. Randy offers opportunities to name your own feelings and realities in the process of becoming your best self."

Lester Laminack

"When breakups happen, our task is to learn and grow through the pain and fear and to awaken to our own truth. (In this book) Randy Siegel charts a course through his own breakup with candor and grace and shines a light for others to see the way through their own dark times. This book is packed with insights and tools to help you find your way back to your inherent divinity. Even if you think you're over your ex, this book can help you learn what your relationship patterns have been so you awaken into loving yourself more fully. The awakened Self is the Divine You that calls out to be a full participant in your next relationship."

The Reverend DiAnna Ritola

"Ladies, Randy Siegel is the guy we've wished for since the days of *Will and Grace*, the fabulous gay best friend. He's that guy who gets us, who loves us enough to tell the truth, and actually wants to hear our stories. Randy gives us a unique masculine perspective, and he's not afraid to share in our breakup sorrow and frustrated nights with Ben and Jerry."

Kathy Godfrey

"Randy's book is easy reading on a hard topic. The reader finds a friend, as Randy openly shares his personal journey through heartbreak in a way that is honest, insightful, and hopeful. I felt like I was sitting across from the author having coffee, as he tells poignant and sometimes funny stories of getting through the messy reality of going through a breakup. Randy distills his experience into teachable moments and wise guidance. His gentle invitations to growth provide a roadmap out of anguish and into a deeper, richer life. I highly recommend!"

Laura Collins

"I can't think of a better friend than Randy, especially when you're going through something as difficult as a breakup. In *Break Up, Wake Up, Move On*, Randy offers readers a delicious cocktail of compassion blended with inspiration and practical 'how to' advice. Most importantly, he shows us how to transform one of life's more crummy moments into gold."

Cheri Britton

"Few authors get our need for connection like Randy Siegel. He's a masterful storyteller, boldly sharing his own experiences to teach us to build better lives. Navigating a relationship split with Randy's concept of conscious parting is brilliant. Whether it's a romantic split, moving away from a 'frenemy,' or setting boundaries with a toxic family member, this book needs to be in your toolbox!"

Elizabeth Vaeth

"Randy's willingness to explore his long-held faulty belief that he was unworthy of love will inspire readers to begin their own inner exploration of Self. The author empowers readers by wisely reminding them that true healing first begins with Self, and that as we heal within we will attract relationships that reflect the unconditional love we offer ourselves."

David B. Robertson, MRHT

"When a relationship ends and it's time to move on, there's a way to move forward in a conscious, loving way; Randy Siegel's book will help you learn how to do this. I've known Randy for years and I've sought his advice on many occasions because he is, simultaneously, supremely practical while being spiritually wise. It is this blending of spiritual wisdom and practical step-by-step procedures that makes Randy's message in this book so wonderful."

Tom Heck

"This is Randy Siegel's best book yet! I will read it over and over to remember the power of authenticity and presence. Thank you, Randy, for sharing your break-up and wake-up experience in an honest and humorous way that will help us move from awareness to awakening in all areas of our lives."

Adair Cates

Contents

Part Three: Wake Up

Part Four: Breakthrough

Part Five: Move On

Appendices: Toolbox

"What is REAL?" asked the Rabbit one day, when they were lying side by side near the nursery fender, before Nana came to tidy the room. "Does it mean having things that buzz inside you and a stick-out handle?"

"Real isn't how you are made," said the Skin Horse. "It's a thing that happens to you. When a child loves you for a long, long time, not just to play with, but REALLY loves you, then you become Real."

"Does it hurt?" asked the Rabbit.

"Sometimes," said the Skin Horse, for he was always truthful. "When you are Real you don't mind being hurt."

"Does it happen all at once, like being wound up," he asked, "or bit by bit?"

"It doesn't happen all at once," said the Skin Horse. "You become. It takes a long time. That's why it doesn't happen often to people who break easily, or have sharp edges, or who have to be carefully kept. Generally, by the time you are Real, most of your hair has been loved off, and your eyes drop out and you get loose in your joints and very shabby. But these things don't matter at all, because once you are Real you can't be ugly, except to people who don't understand."

"I suppose you are real?" said the Rabbit. And then he wished he had not said it, for he thought the Skin Horse might be sensitive. But the Skin Horse only smiled.

"The Boy's Uncle made me Real," he said. "That was a great many years ago; but once you are Real you can't become unreal again. It lasts for always."

The Rabbit sighed. He thought it would be a long time before this magic called Real happened to him. He longed to become Real, to know what it felt like; and yet the idea of growing shabby and losing his eyes and whiskers was rather sad. He wished that he could become it without these uncomfortable things happening to him.

The Velveteen Rabbit: Or How Toys Become Real
by Margery Williams

Preface

A while back, a girlfriend suggested that my next book should be on relationships. Relationships! I had to laugh. For years I was not able to hold on to a relationship for more than three years. And yet… My life's mission is to "help people stand in their power by becoming the full expression of all they are." Love and work are where our inner challenges become most visible, and together they offer the richest soil for growing into our full potential. I've written extensively about work, but little about relationships. My girlfriend was right: that needed to change.

I've now got a lot to say about love, and I can think of no better place to begin that than with a breakup. It's during this painful time that with awareness, attention, and intention, broken hearts become open hearts, and we begin preparing for the partner we've always longed for.

You Are Not Alone

Have you recently been divorced, broken up, or are you still having trouble getting over a past relationship? Do you feel raw, vulnerable, and lonely? Do you spend more time by yourself and tear up while watching the most benign television shows? Perhaps you flinch at the most innocent comments. Do you miss him or her so much that your stomach aches, yet if you were to see him you'd feel as if you'd been sucker punched in the belly? If so, I've been there too. I'm Randy Siegel, and I want to help you get through this.

Regardless of whether you're a guy or girl, I have a good idea of what you're feeling. I struggled with a breakup from a man I was with for three years—the first person I had lived with since my divorce. I went through the breakup with my eyes wide open, and I'd like to share with you what I learned in the hope that it will help you.

I have to be honest. Trying to capture my experience is a little like trying to catch a greased pig. From week to week, I experienced new feelings, thoughts, and insights. But that's behind me, and now I know how to break up, wake up, and move on with more attention, intention, and grace.

In this book, you'll learn:

- While everyone's process is different, you are not alone. None of us gets through life without experiencing loss, but as the Skin Horse explained to the rabbit in *The Velveteen Rabbit*, "Sometimes, when you are Real you don't mind being hurt."

- You will get through this. Whether you get to the other side wiser and ready for a healthier and happier relationship, or sad, disillusioned, and bitter depends on you—and your willingness to do the homework.

- It's during these times of transition that you have the greatest opportunities for growth. Embrace this process and you'll become more aligned with the person you were born to be and with the life you were born to live. I did, and you can too. I'll show you how.

If you're looking for a silver bullet to take away the pain and rush this process, this book is not for you. No book, program, guide, or guru can deliver on such a promise. To become whole and happy takes work, but you don't have to do it alone. I am with you. I hope that by sharing my experience—and the experiences of my girl and guy friends—you'll gain inspiration, insight, and tools to help you get to the other side.

I've divided this book into five parts:

Part One: Setting the Scene
Part Two: Break Up
Part Three: Wake Up
Part Four: Breakthrough
Part Five: Move On

In the appendices, I've included tools that I found particularly helpful. They include: seven commandments for conscious parting; ten tools to help you navigate breaking up, waking up, and moving on; and twelve questions that will help you as you move from breakup to breakthrough. I've also included several additional resources to guide you along your journey. Oh, and one last note about the book: I've changed the names of my ex-partners and friends in order to protect their privacy.

Elizabeth Lesser writes in her wonderful book *Broken Open, How Difficult Times Can Help Us Grow*, "If we can stay awake when our lives are changing, secrets will be revealed to us—secrets about ourselves, about the nature of life, and about the eternal source of happiness and peace that is always available, renewable, already within us."

Most breakups are awful. But with compassion, attention, introspection, and intention they can become transforming, bringing you closer to alignment with your true self while preparing you for the next great adventure. "A breakup can be a kind of rite of passage helping you connect to the person you are now when you consciously go through it," my friend Ann says. The best spiritual teacher is always the life that you are living right now. Yet sometimes in order to learn the lessons of the present, you must first revisit the past.

Part One

Setting the Scene

At the end of my sixth grade year at the Westminster Schools in Atlanta, our class published a newsletter. I remember little about the newspaper other than an article that predicted where each of our classmates would be after the year 2000. For me, they wrote, "Randy Siegel will still be trying to give away his ID bracelet." Little did I know then just how accurate their prediction would be.

Mainstream Married Man

I met the woman I would later marry at a charity ball in Atlanta. Even though we clicked instantly, it took me a month to ask her out. I was afraid she would say no. I couldn't believe my luck when she agreed to go out with me. She was beautiful. I still remember the dress she wore on our first date, and how it made her blue eyes even bluer. I was smitten.

I broke it off several months later fearing our relationship was too superficial. While we had a lot of fun, we rarely had deep, meaningful conversations. I wanted more. But time passed and I began missing her. I thought I had made a mistake by breaking off the relationship. She was pretty, witty, and social. No one had it all, I reasoned, and I could talk about spiritual matters with my friends.

About that time, one of my best friends came out admitting his homosexuality. I was supportive, but was not ready to admit that I too was gay. I'd been aware of my own sexual preferences for as long as I could remember, but I thought I could control, or even outgrow, them. My positive self-image depended on being a mainstream married man.

When I turned twenty-five, it was time to settle down. Most of my friends were married, and I was sure I had found "the One." When I first proposed, she said she wasn't ready. The second time I proposed, she was.

Close to a hundred friends witnessed our marriage on Kentucky Derby weekend in 1981. Our wedding was held at St. Luke's Episcopal

Church in downtown Atlanta, and the reception was on the patio of the Piedmont Driving Club. It was one heck of a party! Our friends still laugh at how much fun they had.

On our honeymoon night, my bride awoke to find I wasn't in our bed. I was staring out the window, lost in thought. I was a homosexual man now trapped in a heterosexual marriage, but I had made a commitment and I had to keep it. It would take every bit of discipline, control, and denial I could garner to live a "normal" married man's life. She never asked, and I never told her what I was thinking that night. It was a covenant that we would keep for the next fourteen years.

Midlife Crisis

At thirty-eight, I called it a midlife crisis. Blaming work for my unhappiness, I complained I had no purpose in my life. I made appointments with two counselors, an industrial psychologist and a psychiatrist. The psychologist gave me the Myers-Briggs test, and concluded my current job was perfect. The psychiatrist dug deeper and suggested I was searching for something more. He began to ask me pointed questions, and before I knew it I told him I was gay.

My secret was out. By admitting it to someone else, I admitted it to myself. There was no going back. Sensing my panic, he assured me that my wife and I would survive. Later when he asked how I felt about living an inauthentic life, I knew I had to do something. I had always prided myself on my honesty and integrity, and I could now see I had been living a lie.

I took a step to remedy this after a Memorial Day weekend trip to the Caribbean, and it was the hardest thing I'd ever done. Gathering all my courage, I blurted out to my wife that I was gay. While she had known something was wrong, she had never suspected my sexuality. Suddenly it all made sense. Fearful for the future and angry about the past, we found our present steeped in pain. We held onto each other on the sofa, and for the first time experienced true intimacy. We pledged to help each other through this, and became each other's chief means of support.

Six weeks later, I moved out. It was her suggestion, and I agreed, wanting her to feel she had some control over her life. What she didn't know was that I had signed a lease on a new place two days earlier.

Serial Monogamist

O pening the door to my new apartment, I faced my greatest fear. After fourteen years of marriage, I was single again. I had moved from a 3,500-square-foot home to an apartment so small that friends dubbed it the "penalty box." Despite the apartment's modest size, it was my sanctuary. It became a place of introspection, healing, and growth.

That first night, I tossed and turned, staring into the darkness. I was not used to sleeping alone. Eyes wide open, I clutched my pillow and waited for morning. "There will be light," my older brother advised. "But you have to walk through the darkness to get to it."

Several months later, I was divorced and free to date. Going out with man after man, I felt like an Atlanta debutante at her coming-out party. Fresh and not jaded, I was the belle of the ball. I cruised bars, danced at discos, and vacationed at the gay meccas of South Beach, Provincetown, and Palm Springs. At first, it was fun being single, but after a while I grew bored. I was ready to settle down.

In 1998 I moved to Asheville, North Carolina, and enjoyed a series of one-to-three-year relationships, including one with a woman (she remains one of my closest friends today). "I don't know what's wrong with me," I said to a friend. "Why can't I find a long-term partner?" "Maybe you're a serial monogamist," he suggested. While that may have been true, it didn't feel like enough.

4

Stop the Pain!

In 2005, I hit a dry spell. I had work I loved, a home I was proud of, money in the bank, and a comforting cadre of loving friends. But it still wasn't enough. Despite the rich trappings of my life, I felt like a pauper. I had no partner. A clawing hunger consumed my soul and no matter how hard I tried to feed it—by doing, being, analyzing, bargaining, settling, repressing, and running—the pain continued to haunt me.

When I was growing up, my father said, "You can be anything, do anything, or have anything you want, son, if you just want it bad enough." Dad lied, for there was nothing in the world I wanted more than a lover—yet I was alone. Did I want it too much? Had desire swelled into obsession, and had obsession squeezed out all hope of a special someone coming into my life?

The tapes played in my head:

You will always be alone.

You're not good enough.

You don't deserve love.

I was now over fifty. Would I always be alone? The pool of available men was getting smaller, and I couldn't afford to lose my looks to age. I lived alone. I worked alone. I felt isolated.

Several times a day I picked up the phone to check my voice mail. It was empty. My mailbox was full of bills, and my e-mail was cluttered with junk mail. I longed for connection. Feeling empty, I prayed for The White Knight to save me from myself.

Self-help books said I should love myself. Religion preached I am never alone, and therapists counseled that only I can make myself whole. But no one could tell me how. No one could tell me how to ease this pain. I tried to take care of myself. I wrote in my journal, walked, meditated, and worked out. For brief moments I'd forget, but within minutes the longing would return. It always returned.

Embrace the Pain

"Embrace the pain," the self-help books counsel. "With pain comes growth."

I tried their advice. A single tear ran down my face while a river of emotion flowed through my veins. Is my pain too deep? Will it ever surface?

I found no comfort among friends who shared my loneliness. They only mirrored my pain and the absurdity of my actions. I was self-absorbed and needy, yet I gave advice. "No partner will be attracted to such desperation," I warned. I removed the splinter from their eye while a log was lodged in my own. Charged by the electric buzz of my friends' restlessness, I fought to stay grounded. Desperation clung to them like cheap cologne. I pledged not to join them on another frantic, manic manhunt, yet I remained on several Internet dating sites.

I ran from one relationship to another. Few lasted more than a couple of months. At first, I blamed these men: "None of them were right for me." Finally, I looked within. "What am I doing wrong?" I asked. I berated myself. "If only I was less intense, more giving, less judgmental, less dependent…." "If only…" If only…"

And the tapes continued to play in my head:

You're not good enough.

You don't deserve love.

You will always be alone.

My ex-wife's words haunted me. "I hope one day you'll know the pain I feel," she said. I was cursed. Sentenced to a solitary life, my loneliness was my punishment for the pain I caused her.

You don't deserve love.

You're not good enough.

You will always be alone.

The tapes cycled through their endless loop, and I wanted them to stop. I knew that awareness is the first step to recovery. I sought to understand. I found healing by asking what purpose these mind messages served. What was the payoff and what was the cost? Perhaps these tapes protected me from love. By avoiding love, I avoided the possibility of getting hurt. The tapes denied me the very thing I wanted most in life.

I'd had enough. I cried out:

I will find love!

I am enough!

I do deserve love!

I am ready.

Manhunt

While I'm a little embarrassed to admit it, I used to believe in fairy tales. I sought The White Knight to save me, or The Good Mother to soothe my wounds. There's a scene in the movie *Jerry Maguire* where Jerry turns to Dorothy and says, "I love you. You complete me." I used to believe that it takes two halves to make a whole, and I was willing to search the world to find my missing half.

No one could have been more strategic. I enlisted a coach, signed up on several online dating services, and rented a small apartment in Washington, D.C., to expand my social network. I even built a small altar in the foyer of my home to attract my future mate. I began as the books advised:

I wrote an ideal partner description. I was as detailed as I dared.

Tall, thin, and in shape

Within four years of my age

Spiritual

Smart

Kind

Gentle

Considerate

The list went on. One day I had an epiphany: this detailed inventory provided far more value than a simple wish list describing the characteristics I sought in a soul mate — it represented the disowned aspects of my self waiting to be reclaimed. For example, I wrote that I was seeking someone gentle yet strong, someone who could take over the reins when I am tired so I don't have to be so hyper vigilant coordinating all the details of life. I now know my happiness does not depend on finding this person. In fact, I did date several men who embodied just these characteristics, and found it still wasn't enough. **Instead, I discovered that my happiness depends on assimilating these (and other) attributes from my ideal partner profile into my personality.**

Assimilation begins with awareness, and it requires patience. I began to see myself as a man who is both gentle and strong, but I still caught myself longing for that special someone to take over the steering wheel for a while. When I did, I reminded myself that this is one of the lessons I am here to learn: how to be less hyper vigilant and more trusting of life.

I've heard it said that we cannot love another until we love ourselves. While I understood this intellectually, I didn't get it on a gut level. A friend put it more bluntly, "You leave this world alone. Unless you enjoy the company while you're here, it's not going to be a fun ride."

I learned that I enjoyed my own company. I liked going out to eat by myself and with myself, and I liked traveling alone at times. The more I enjoyed my company, the less dependent I became on a relationship; and the less I clung to having to be in a relationship, the more likely I was to attract one into my life. I stopped searching for that magic potion, silver bullet, or golden apple that would manifest the ideal partner, and focused on becoming the best person I could be and living the best life I could.

> **Consider This: List three attributes you'd like in an ideal partner that perhaps you've disowned in yourself.**

The Dance

I met "Christopher" in Provincetown, Massachusetts, a well-known beach resort on Cape Cod outside of Boston. I had been in Boston for business. It was around my birthday, and I decided to treat myself to several days on the Cape. One of Provincetown's traditions is the afternoon tea dance at the Boatslip. After sunning on the beach one day, I decided to go. I love to dance.

Standing on the edge of the dance floor, a handsome man caught my eye. Was he smiling at me? At me? What was wrong? This guy was so handsome; he was way out of my league. He continued to look my way and smile. What did I have to lose? I introduced myself.

We talked, and he asked me to dance. We danced, and we talked some more. He was much younger than me. He was twenty-nine, and I was fifty-one. We had little in common, but damn was he handsome! And smart too. I asked him to dinner. He responded that he had been in Provincetown for almost two weeks, but was planning to drive home to Connecticut after tea dance. He then hesitated for a moment: "But I can always go a little later. I'd love to go to dinner."

We continued to talk; our conversation got deeper, and after a second martini I got bolder. "My fantasy is that you'd spend the night and go home tomorrow morning." He smiled an impish grin and nodded yes. Two days later, he left for Connecticut. Four days later, I returned to the mountains of North Carolina.

8

Moving In

Despite the distance, we continued our courtship. Intellectually it made no sense. I was old enough to be his father. We came from very different backgrounds, we shared few interests, and Christopher was out of work. Despite all of this, we had what I can only describe as a karmic connection. I had this inner knowing that we were meant to be together.

Christopher came to visit for two weeks and then again for two months. Not too long after that, we packed up a rented U-haul and moved Christopher to the South. I was excited, and I was frightened. One of the hardest parts of becoming part of a couple was letting go of my identity as a single person. I strongly identified with the archetype of "the seeker." In my work, I seek knowledge about leadership and communications, and in my spiritual life I seek the truth. I also enjoyed seeking as a single person. I loved the hunt; I even loved the dating "dance." But Christopher was worth it.

In preparation, I cleared out space for him. I packed up my down-stairs painting studio so that he would have his own office, and I cleared out closet and drawer space. Finally, I cleared out psychic space so that he'd have a place in my heart. One way I did this was reading through old journals, especially those sections I wrote regarding past relationships. Some of this reading was painful. I realized I had much to learn about being in an intimate relationship.

I wanted to show up in the relationship—warts and all; I wanted to show Christopher all of me. This meant clearly stating my needs before they became resentments. It also meant letting go of any expectations that he would meet them. I knew Christopher couldn't meet all my needs—no one could. It would be up to me to address those needs.

I wanted to give Christopher what I wanted most in life: unconditional love. Well, maybe not *unconditional* love, but pretty darn close to it. I didn't want to change him; I wanted to accept him as he was. I'd been around enough to know that often it's the differences we love about our partner that later become irritants. I wanted to continue to love those differences, rather than convert them. I also wanted to remember that Christopher had his own spiritual path. I had no right to try to guide him or worse, to shape him. Being a born coach and consultant, this was going to be tough, but I pledged to be strong in my resolve.

I told myself that it didn't matter whether our relationship lasted for a week, several months, or a lifetime. I knew that relationships are the great classrooms of life, and I was ready to learn. I began the relationship with the best of intentions—but sometimes good intentions are not enough.

Part Two

Breakup

Over the next three years, I learned a great deal about myself and being in relationship. Some insights included:

- I hate conflict and tend to do whatever it takes to smooth things over.

- I wasn't as good a communicator as I had thought. I had a hard time initiating a candid conversation about something as simple as how our relationship was going. Such a conversation seemed scary. I was afraid I'd open up a can of worms, and he would express his unhappiness and leave me.

- I could be loving and affectionate. I show my love by doing.

- I enjoyed sharing meals, my space, and life with someone significant.

As the relationship matured, we grew farther apart instead of closer. The relationship was malnourished, and by the third year, it was starving. I wrote in my journal, "It is spring, yet it feels like winter. Despite the beauty that surrounds me, I am sad." Spring is normally one of my favorite seasons, but that year it became a season of sadness. As beautiful as budding trees were, I was ready for them to drop their leaves. I longed to see bare branches stripped to their essence, for only then could new growth begin.

9

The Split

It's been said that no one dies from a broken heart, but I wasn't convinced. It felt like death to me. Christopher moved out in May. No one was to blame; we had simply grown apart. I wondered what happened. Was it the age difference? There were twenty-two years between us. Or was it different values and interests? While all these factors probably contributed to our split, I believe that we simply didn't put enough energy into the relationship.

I now see that when a couple gets together, there are three entities at play: there's you, your partner, and the relationship. Our relationship didn't get the love, care, and feeding it needed to survive.

My intention was to manage our separation with as much love and grace as I could muster. Our last dinner together was poignant and painful. Christopher presented me with a beautiful card. As I opened it, three dried rose petals fell to the floor. "When you flew to Connecticut to help move me to Asheville, you gave me a single white rose," he began. "I dried six petals and pressed them in my journal. Tonight, I'm returning three." Ritual complete, the relationship was over.

Christopher moved out several days later while I was away in Los Angeles on business. We planned it that way. I felt it would be too painful to be there when he left the house for the last time. In dream language, houses stand for psyche.

When I returned from Los Angeles, I performed a ritual to take back possession of the house. I went from room to room visualizing a happy moment spent with Christopher. In each room, I burned sage, sprinkled salt and water, and lit incense. As I left the room, I turned off the light and whispered, "I release you in love and light."

No Contact

Before Christopher left, I told him I needed time to heal, and wanted no contact. **A sentence must have a period before a new sentence can begin.** A month later, he called. It was an awkward conversation. He wanted to get together. I told him I wasn't ready. A month later, he called again. I told him once again I wasn't ready. Maybe in the fall, I'd be okay with seeing him.

When my birthday rolled around in August, he sent a card and an expensive bar of soap In the fall he called again, and I still wasn't ready. "If you'll only meet with me once, I'll stop calling," he promised tearfully. I said no. The thought of meeting was just too painful.

A month later, he called again; I was firmer, "Stop calling me," I said. "No contact means no contact, and I want no contact!" I had discovered my anger, and it felt empowering. "Ever?" he asked. "Forever is a long time," I said tersely. "All I can tell you is that for now I want no contact. Do not call me again."

11

Party Pooper

Several weeks later, two friends invited me to a dinner party for a mutual friend who was in town. I accepted and asked if I could bring a date. "Of course," they said. My date had a last-minute conflict, and I went alone.

Driving up to their house, I felt something was wrong. At the door I was greeted warmly by my hosts. I turned the corner and there in the living room was Christopher talking to a small group. I started shaking. I felt ambushed. Not wanting to cause a scene, I plastered on a smile and warmly greeted each of the guests including my ex. We awkwardly hugged. My heart was pounding so hard that I wondered if he could feel it through my shirt.

I poured a glass of wine and mingled. My legs were still shaking, but no one would have known it. When one of the hosts went back into the kitchen to prepare our meal, I followed him. "I am sorry, but I'm very uncomfortable," I began. "This is very painful for me to be with my ex-partner. I wanted to let you know that I'm going to slip out a little later." "Oh?" my host began. "We love you both and figured the group was large enough that you'd be okay." "I totally understand," I said. The last thing I wanted to do was to make my host uncomfortable. This was my problem, not his. "I hope you'll at least stay for dinner," he continued. "I'll do my best," I promised.

An hour later, dinner was served. As the guests lined up for the buffet, I discreetly tiptoed to the coat closet to retrieve my jacket. Suddenly, the booming voice of my host filled the entry hall. "You aren't leaving us!" Within seconds, my hosts, the guest of honor, and my ex-partner had surrounded me. Some of the guests came out of the kitchen to see what the commotion was about.

I was humiliated. Murmuring that I needed to leave, I stumbled out the door and hurried down the walkway to my car. The guest of honor trailed me. Still trying to be polite, I apologized over my shoulder. "I am so sorry," I said. "I know you like us both." I'm not sure what else I said, but I managed to get in my car and drive off. I felt as if I were going to throw up.

That night, I didn't sleep. As I tossed and turned, my heart continued to pound and my head was spinning. You could have filled a book with the stories I crafted about what was said after my departure.

Randy is pining away without Christopher...

I can't believe how rude Randy was...

I never knew how fragile Randy is...

I was hurt. I was angry. I felt alone.

"I know there's learning in this," I confided to a close friend. "But for the life of me, I can't find my way clear to see it." I was having crazy thoughts and roller-coaster emotions.

12

Crazy Thoughts

Looking back, I must have thought that I could think my way through the breakup. Now I see just how wrong I was. My head was filled with compulsions and fantasies. If I wasn't thinking about the past, I was worrying about the future.

I wonder what he told his mother and friends up north about our breakup. How will I feel and how will I react when I see Christopher out on a date? Does he have any regrets, or is he just relieved we are through?

While the relationship was clearly over, I just couldn't get Christopher out of my head.

Compulsions

One of the first studies to examine the brains of the recently broken-hearted reported that losing a lover has the same effect on the brain as trying to kick an intense addiction. After reading that participants spent more than 85 percent of their waking hours thinking about their lost love, I felt better. Maybe I wasn't as crazy as I thought.

I would see a red car and check to see if it was Christopher's.

I would pass a restaurant and remember a special dinner we had shared there.

I would think about a trip we had talked about but never got around to taking.

I started to notice that my thoughts grouped into four archetypes: victim, child, saboteur, and whore. Like four flavors on a snow cone, my thoughts tasted different depending on which archetype I chose at the time.

The victim loved playing the martyr. He placed blame on my ex and took little responsibility. It was one of the few times that I was actually compassionate towards myself.

He withdrew from the relationship. He spent more time on the computer than with me.

He took all I did for him for granted.

I was his ticket to Asheville.

Little of it was true, but that made no difference to the victim.

When I chose the archetype of the child, I felt helpless and vulnerable.

I can't make it without Christopher.

What will I do when:

- *I have a technology issue?*
- *I have to drive on a long trip?*
- *I have to protect myself?*

The saboteur had to admit that he was partially responsible for the demise of the relationship. That was easy; I'm pretty hard on myself.

I zoned out. I wasn't present enough during our relationship.

I wasn't affectionate enough.

I became his coach—and at times his father. I didn't view or treat him as an equal partner.

I didn't speak up about my needs.

The whore ranted about the times that I compromised my true nature in order to stay in the relationship:

I tolerated some totally unacceptable behavior.

I spent time with people I didn't enjoy.

I shrank.

My mind was on overdrive with compulsive thinking, which served as a defense against the powerful emotions I refused to feel. "Face it, you're obsessive, Randy," a friend observed. "You used to be obsessive about your business; now it's about Christopher. After Christopher, it will be something—or someone—else.

"Instead of asking yourself why you're obsessing about Christopher, perhaps it'd be more valuable to ask why you obsess in the first place," he said. I didn't have a clue. "Do you want a suggestion?" he asked. "Of course." He then made a powerful one: "Maybe you're obsessing as a way of avoiding the present." He had made his point.

Fantasies

Observing my mind-talk, I was surprised at how often my thoughts grew into tall stories. In one, Christopher desperately missed me and wanted to get back together. In another he was actively dating and had totally forgotten about me. At times, I would even tell myself our breakup was only temporary. A girlfriend set me straight. "You've been thinking that getting back together is impossible," she said. "I'd like you to entertain that it's not." She continued, "Jump into the fantasy that you're reunited and see how you feel."

I took her advice, and afterwards felt like I'd been sprayed with cold water. There was no going back. We had split for a reason, and that reason had not changed. Going back to your ex is a fantasy many entertain after a breakup—no matter how bad the relationship was. Most agree it's a bad idea. **"Putting sour milk back in the fridge doesn't make it drinkable again,"** my friend Kelli says.

Past and Future Tense

Most of my thoughts were built on past memories or an imagined future. Some memories were pleasant; others were not. Most of my future imaginings were fear-based. I feared being alone or, more specifically, I feared being lonely. I know there's a big difference between the two. Being alone was one thing, but the loneliness… I found this poem by the fourteenth century Persian poet, Hafiz:

Don't surrender your loneliness
So quickly
Let it cut deep.

Let it ferment and season you
As few human
Or even divine ingredients can.

Something missing in my heart tonight
Has made my eyes so soft,
My voice
So tender,

My need for God
Absolutely
Clear.

The poem was lovely, but could I stand the pain if I allowed loneliness to cut so deep? I wasn't sure. Funny. After Christopher left, I don't remember feeling lonely. Thank heavens for friends. My friends listened to me patiently, and more than once they set me straight.

My mind was in constant motion spitting out thoughts faster than a Diet Coke machine at a sorority house. Thoughts are said to trigger emotions—it's no wonder mine were all over the place.

> **Consider This: List as many of the crazy thoughts that have been going through your head as you can. Include compulsions, fantasies, memories, and projections. Sometimes it helps just to get them on paper.**

13

Roller-Coaster Emotions

I n their book, *On Grief and Grieving: Finding the Meaning of Grief through the Five Stages of Loss,* Elisabeth Kübler-Ross and David Kessler identify the five stages of grieving:

1. Denial
2. Anger
3. Bargaining
4. Depression
5. Acceptance

Kübler-Ross and Kessler wrote that these steps don't necessarily come in order, nor are all the steps experienced by everyone, though most people experience at least two. I skipped denial and bargaining but went back for second helpings of depression and anger. Compared to sadness, anger was delicious. At least with anger, I didn't feel so helpless.

Most people mix a custom cocktail using a combination of these emotions:

- Hurt and Sadness
- Anger and Blame
- Fear and Insecurity
- Remorse and Responsibility
- Understanding and Empathy
- Love, Forgiveness, and Appreciation

Whatever the emotional path, it's not likely to be a linear one. We can feel many emotions at the same time.

So much for the love and grace I exhibited when we first ended the relationship. Like a kaleidoscope, love turned into relief, relief into sadness, sadness into anger, anger into jealousy, and jealousy back into love.

Love

I pictured Christopher, and I softened. I saw his beauty, his intellect, and his innocence. I remembered why I fell in love with him. While his looks initially attracted me, it was his mind that really captured me. I loved how he thought, and admired how he constantly wrestled with the "whys." I also loved that spirituality was important to him, and I appreciated our age difference. He brought out the "young man" in me, and I tried to help him feel safe, smart, and capable of accomplishing whatever it was he wanted from life. I loved when he put his hand on my thigh when I drove. I loved when he hugged me for no reason, and I loved snuggling with him at night.

He was gentle, sweet, and caring. I appreciated that he was conscious of paying his way. Money was not important to him. Sometimes, it's too important to me. I experienced a familiarity with him—like being with an old friend or long-term lover. Perhaps we had been together in a past life. I believe true love is eternal. Once I have loved someone—regardless of how much anger or hurt I might have felt—I never stop loving that person.

Relief

"Randy, it's okay to admit that you're relieved," Joseph suggested. Joseph is Joseph Dispenza, author of *God on Your Own: Finding a Spiritual Path Outside Religion* (and many other books). Joseph and I met twice a month by phone to analyze my dreams. I had just shared a slew of dreams in which a celebration was taking place, and once again Joseph had hit the nail on the head. Although I hadn't admitted it to myself, I was relieved that the relationship was over. Looking back, Christopher and I had been living separate lives.

On most weekends, Christopher would go out on Saturday night after dinner and stay out dancing until two and three o'clock in the morning. Additionally, he had met a new group of friends and was hesitant to introduce me. I had told myself it was okay; he was just trying to build his own network. But in truth, I felt hurt.

On my part, I took an apartment in New York for three weeks in December. Christopher visited, but I didn't invite him to stay the full three weeks. That summer, I planned to rent another Manhattan apartment for five months. Again, Christopher was invited to visit but not stay.

Yes, I was relieved; I was glad it was over, but that didn't mean I wasn't sad too.

Sadness

Even though I knew that breaking up was the right thing, I hurt—and I hate pain. In the past, I would have accelerated my activities to numb it. But this time I didn't. I sat with the pain. Don't get me wrong, I wanted it to pass—and pass quickly—but I also wanted to feel it this time. I knew it was the only way I could get through this with all of me intact.

Life isn't always sunshine and butterflies. Life is duality; it is "both-and." Darkness follows light, and death follows life. It's unrealistic to think that happiness comes by being happy all the time. True happiness comes through contentment, and contentment is found in gently accepting "what is."

I visualized my pain. It looked like a rat's nest—a tight ball of string, wire, dust, dirt, and broken pieces of metal and glass. It was dense. When pressed, it slowly and stubbornly sprang back into place. That's how I envisioned my "pain-body." In his book, *A New Earth: Awakening to Your Life's Purpose,* Eckhart Tolle defines the pain-body as remnants of pain left behind by every strong negative emotion we have not fully faced, accepted, and then let go. As an energy field, it demands to be fed periodically, and it feeds on negative thinking.

After our separation, my pain-body was on a ravenous binge. I was in a nasty mood, and I wasn't able to shake it. The death of our relationship had been a slow one. Pain bodies love drama. To the pain-body, pain is pleasure. I blamed Christopher, then I blamed myself:

The writing was on the wall. Why did I choose not to read it?
I should have ended it a long time ago.
If only, I had…then he would have…
The snakes in my head hissed on.

In a sick way, I enjoyed it. Martyrdom is one of the few times I am compassionate with myself.

I wanted the pain-body to go away, but it lingered. "What we resist, persists," the maxim says. Tolle suggests that the way out of the pain-body is awareness, acceptance, and presence. "The beginning of freedom from the pain-body lies first of all in the realization that you *have* a pain-body."

When I tuned into my pain-body, I was less identified with it. I still felt unhappy, but I was not that unhappiness. It was as if I was observing myself being unhappy. I began to listen to the negative stories I crafted and realized they weren't based in reality. Sometimes I shouted, "Stop!" But the stories kept rolling on like an endless loop of film. I tried to relax, observe, and feel what I was feeling.

When I was conscious of the stories, I was less likely to be reactive. Pain-bodies depend on unconsciousness to exist. Pain-bodies also depend on the past and the future. "When we become totally present, pain-bodies become dormant," Tolle writes. He is probably right, but I wasn't successful. I hadn't yet learned how to stay present.

Over time pain-bodies loosen their grip. It's then we can break up the dense mass of unexamined thoughts and emotions, emotional thinking, and story-making that form the heart of the pain-body.

Anger

He made fun of my sagging chin and the fact that I'm aging.

I did almost everything around the house, including meal planning and cooking.

He thought holidays were frivolous. One Christmas, he didn't even give me a gift until two weeks after the holiday.

Before I knew it, I had listed forty-seven entries in my journal detailing why I was angry with Christopher. Looking back on them now, more than 60 percent were self-directed. Was my anger justified? Probably not. But I was still angry.

"You have every right to be angry, Randy," my friend Ginger snapped. "The SOB cheated on you!" Ginger was right. Towards the end of the relationship, Christopher stepped out on me. Although it happened only once, it was the straw that broke the camel's back. In truth, his tryst reflected what was already happening in the relationship. But it still hurt, and it made me angry.

He never took responsibility for his actions—much less apologized for hurting me.

After all I did for him!

I saw it coming. Why didn't I put a stop to it?

I tried to be gentle with myself. Wasn't anger one of the stages of grieving? And there's something empowering about righteous indignation. Instead of being shamed by it, I decided to enjoy it—at least for a while.

Jealousy, Hatred, and Vindictiveness

I thought of Christopher enjoying his new group of friends, and my stomach knotted. I thought of Christopher dating, and I cringed. If I couldn't be with him, no one should. I caught myself speaking ill of him to a mutual friend and stopped in mid-sentence. What kind of person had I become? "Don't feel bad, Randy. It's normal," my friend Anna soothed. **"Hatred and vindictiveness can run as deep as the love you once held."**

Over time, my less-than-pure thoughts and occasional rude comments came less often, and when they did I tried to listen, observe, and reserve judgment. Sometimes I even found compassion for myself. I knew that I was acting out of fear. I learned that it's important to not mask these emotions, but to feel them. Laura, my friend who is a poet, reminded me of the wise words of Rumi, the thirteenth century mystic: "Find the antidote in the venom."

14

Acting Out

Friends warned me to watch out for unhealthy behavior after my breakup. Despite their warnings, I became obsessed with sex.

"The best way to get over someone is to get under someone else," a woman once told me after her divorce. A fling? Maybe, but what I was doing felt obsessive and not healthy. I couldn't get enough. I had to ask myself why.

I came to the conclusion that I was feeling powerless, and sex was one thing that I felt I could control. A female friend jumped feet first into the singles scene after her breakup. "I knew it was too soon and probably not healthy, but I needed the distraction," she said. "More importantly, I needed a man to tell me I was attractive. After my divorce, my confidence was shot."

"I became obsessed with working out," a guy friend shared. "There are worse ways to deal with a breakup, but I was crazed, spending two to three hours a day at the gym." When I asked another friend how she dealt with her particularly nasty breakup, she smiled and gave a one-word answer: "Wine." Other friends chose food. When my friend Nancy got divorced, she called a company that conducted estate sales and instructed them to: "Sell everything that he touched." From the scissors to the silverware, nothing remained.

After Christopher left, I put my convertible on the market. Thankfully, I pulled the ad a week later. "Don't make any big decisions right after breaking up," advised articles on breaking up. Almost everyone I talked with had sought some strategy to regain a renewed sense of power and avoid dealing with the pain, and many of these strategies were obsessive and unhealthy.

15

Rebound Relationships

Most experts suggest waiting a while before dating again. Otherwise, you're likely headed for a "rebound relationship." I chose to ignore this advice when Thomas came into my life only months after Christopher and I split. Thomas was handsome, creative, considerate, and smart. Best of all, unlike Christopher and me, we shared many common values and interests.

I told myself that I loved Thomas—and I did—but more as a friend than a lover. Time spent with him was more about distraction than attraction. From the beginning, I was clear with Thomas that I was still healing from the demise of my relationship, and he said he understood. I also explained that I was in no place to fully commit to a new relationship. He said he could be patient.

Months later, I admitted that I wasn't ready to be in a relationship. I said to Thomas, "There are three of us in this relationship: you, Christopher, and me." Once again, Thomas understood, and we parted as friends.

16

Be Gentle

My friends were great about reminding me to take care of myself. They suggested that I watch my diet and get plenty of exercise and rest. Regina suggested bodywork. She said, "During my breakup, I loved splurging and booking a massage, facial, or mani-pedi. It was nice just being touched."

Bruce reminded me that a breakup could disrupt almost every area of your life. He suggested, "When everything feels different, take solace in your schedule." Taking Bruce's advice, I awoke every morning at the same time, went to the gym, came home and showered, and started my day. Getting back into a regular routine helped me to feel normal and safe.

Of all the advice I received, the most valuable was to **catch that inner critic before he or she multiplies into an inner committee.**

I should have known better than to date a man so young.

I should have ended it sooner.

I should have...

Inner critics are tough customers to deal with. I've found the best strategy is awareness. When my inner critic reared its ugly, troll-like head, I tried to laugh and say *give me a break!*

During your breakup, expect some less-than-desirable traits to show up in your behavior patterns. I gave mine a label: my "evil twin."

I hope he's miserable without me.

I hope he's missing all the things I used to do for him.

I hope he's regretting…

In the South, most of us have at least one crazy relative. Instead of being ashamed of them, we take their craziness in stride. "You remember Auntie Jane," we might say. "She lived in the attic and didn't come down for years." I've found it's best to treat our evil twin with the same acceptance. **Henry Miller was right when he wrote: "The full and joyful acceptance of the worst may be the only sure way of transforming it."** A shadow is no longer a shadow when it meets the full light of day.

17

Lessons Learned About Breaking Up

- Consider asking your ex for no contact—at least for a while. Allow yourself time to heal and redefine the relationship if you choose to become friends. Remember, "no contact means no contact." Ask your friends not to share information about your ex.

- While everyone's process is different, most people will find their minds working overtime to heighten the drama and avoid being present.

- Expect a gamut of emotions—all coming at the same time. Explore your pain-body.

- Don't try to control or crush crazy thoughts and jumbled feelings—you'll only increase their charge. Instead, simply observe them with curiosity and without judgment, knowing that, like clouds, they'll simply float by.

- It's important to wait a while before acting, as we all have the potential to do some pretty crazy things after a breakup. It also may be helpful to have an accountability partner (or two) to ensure that you don't do something you'll regret later.

- Be fair to yourself and potential partners and postpone dating for a while. Enjoy time spent with friends and yourself.

- Be good to yourself. Be compassionate with yourself. Expect to be obsessed with your breakup for a while. Diffuse the power your inner critic has over you through awareness. Accept your evil twin. Eat well and exercise often. Pamper yourself freely. Get back into a regular routine.

Looking back, I don't think I'd change much about how the breakup happened between Christopher and me. Despite well-meaning friends pushing me to leave the relationship earlier ("Randy, you're just postponing the inevitable."), I had an inner knowing that the right time would present itself—and it did. Our decision to separate was mutual. No one felt left behind.

Part Three

Wake Up

Why was I holding on? It made no sense. I could understand holding on if Christopher was the one who shouldn't have gotten away, but he wasn't. The relationship had run its course. So why was I holding on? Anger? Love? Was I idealizing the relationship? Or was I holding on to the relationship because deep down I hoped that Christopher would make up for the hurt he caused and make things right? Perhaps it was unfinished business. I wasn't able to get him to meet all my needs. If I had only…

STOP! Make these crazy thoughts, roller-coaster emotions, and acting out stop!

Freud taught that underneath every wish is a fear of having that wish come true. If I had caught a leprechaun, waved a wand, or rubbed the magic lantern and made it stop, I would have missed the pot of gold at the end of rainbow. I had to accept and commit to the process of letting go if I was to truly heal and move on.

When you embrace the process, you are called to wake up to yourself and life in this moment. It's only then that you open your eyes, look around, and see the pot of gold that's been there all along; that pot of gold is your authentic self or your divinity.

Several years ago a spiritual guide observed, "Randy, you are extremely aware, but you are not awake." At the time, I wasn't sure what she meant. I am now. While I was aware of all I was going through, I was not awake to the emotions that I was feeling.

18

Suffer Not

I couldn't do it on my own. Friends and family were helpful, but I was concerned about how much I could continue to lean on them—and how objective could they be. There are times in our lives when we need outside help, and this was one of them. A friend gave me the name of a therapist, and I made an appointment. "I think you'll like this guy's approach," she said.

"The first thing you need to know is that this is not about Christopher," he began. My therapist was Leland (Chip) Baggett, author of *Waking Up Together: An Interactive Practice for Couples*. Not about Christopher! Was he nuts? "Randy, life is calling you to go into the space you've spent most of your life avoiding," he continued. "Are you ready?" I had to be honest; I wasn't sure. I wanted to grow, but I was terrified to face the pain.

"Where your 'yes' meets your 'no,' you'll find your growth edge," he said.

It's been said that when the heart breaks open, the true self can be revealed, or as the Skin Horse says in *The Velveteen Rabbit*, you become real. Chip was right: I had spent most of my life avoiding pain, specifically sadness. If I allowed the sadness to seep in, I was afraid it would swallow me, and I'd no longer be able to function. I was frightened that I would literally lose my mind.

"There's a difference between pain and suffering," Chip explained. "You can be in pain, but you don't need to suffer. Pain is sensation; suffering is resistance to the pain."

His words sounded good, but I really didn't understand them. In subsequent sessions, I began to see that Chip was talking about being present. When I can be present to pain without judgment, there's no need to suffer. For example, when I thought about Christopher and felt sad, I could make note that I felt sad. Rather than judging sadness to be a "bad" thing, I could sit with it. Like a train passing through a station, the thought would pass and within minutes the sadness would dissipate.

Chip's wise counsel was helpful, but there were three challenges. First, I didn't want to be present to the pain; I wanted it to go away. Second, I am hugely judgmental. Third, spiritual writer Eckhart Tolle writes that there are three ways the ego treats the present: as a means to an end, an obstacle, or as an enemy. Time had become my enemy.

19

Being and Doing

I am a student of the Enneagram, a personality system that helps explain how we are wired. As an Enneagram "Three," inactivity causes me anxiety. A while back, my business was slow, and time was heavy. To cope, I sped up. I took on new tasks—some productive, most not. I joined a nonprofit organization's board of directors and found enumerable ways to pass time on the computer. I numbed out. I read, watched television, ran errands, and piddled around the house. While there's nothing wrong with these activities, I did them robotically and without joy.

None of these tactics worked. While some offered a temporary respite from anxiety, they also dulled my life. When I disconnect from being, I disconnect from Self, and how can I be authentic and live a joyful life when I am not associated with Self? I can't.

For the first half of my life, I was solely about doing. A friend once observed, "Randy, everything you've accomplished you accomplished by sheer force of will."

My friend was right. I gritted my teeth, rolled up my sleeves, and made things happen, but I did it all unconsciously. While I got a lot done, I was in a trance; I wasn't present. I wasn't present to my work, relationships, or life. That was then. Now I felt ready to put being into my doing.

Five months after my breakup, a flyer arrived in the mail for a seven-day meditation retreat outside of Asheville, and I knew I needed to go. I had experimented with meditation before, but nothing seemed to stick. Now I was in a more receptive place. I followed my intuition and signed up.

20

Becoming Aware

No sex. No meat. No alcohol and no talking. For seven days. "You've got to be out of your mind!" my friends teased. Three days before the meditation retreat, I wondered if they were right. Despite my nervousness, I went.

The first day, twenty-two of us were seated in the large meditation hall warmed by a wood stove. Over the next week, I learned how to separate my thoughts from my Self. Under the constant waves of my thoughts and feelings, I found a calm, still sea. Staying present wasn't as daunting as I had thought. I came to learn that all it requires of us is to tune into our thoughts and feelings, and watch our responses.

I found that thoughts, feelings, fantasies, and sensations pass quickly when recognized and observed. When a painful memory or negative thought arose, I would note it: "Remembrance. Remembrance. Remembrance." "Feeling. Feeling. Feeling." I didn't try to analyze it; only name it. Once named, it eventually would pass. If it lingered, I refocused on my breath. Minutes later, it would dissipate. I was proud of myself: I could meditate!

21

Meditation as a Way of Being

I became a zealot about meditation. "I'm trying to figure out when I can schedule forty-five minutes of meditation five days a week," I enthusiastically proclaimed to my therapist. "May I make a suggestion?" he gently asked. "Of course." "Instead of scheduling another 'to do' on your list, what if you were to practice what you learned at the retreat throughout the day? Meditation is not just another activity. It's a different way of being in the moment you're already in." Chip then proceeded to share a wonderful analogy that I'll never forget.

"Here are a rock, a pond, and a destination across the pond," he began. "Think of the rock as the focus of your attention. The pond is the present moment, and the destination across the pond is an outcome you are seeking. You've spent most of your life skipping that rock across the surface of the pond in order to reach the destination." So far, I was with him. "When you meditate, or tune into your thoughts, it's as if the rock immediately stops skipping across the water. It has no choice but to sink."

He continued. **"Think of awareness as being on a horizontal and vertical axis. At any given moment ask yourself two questions: 'Where is the focus of my attention?' and 'What is the intensity, or depth, of my attention?'"** Those two simple questions changed my life. In them lay the key for how to wake up and become present to my life.

Facing the Past

The more willing I am to face the pain, the more present I become. I have little memory of my childhood. I believe that's because I wasn't present for much of it. It was one of the ways I coped. My parents did the best they could—and they were good parents in many ways—but few of us come through childhood without some wounding.

My deepest wound was that I didn't feel loved for who I was, only for an idealized image of what I should or could be. As a child, I didn't have coping skills to deal with this hurt. In order to protect myself from the present, I retreated to the past or projected into the future. My imagination became the strongest defense against the helplessness I felt.

I read once that you have to nurture the child you were in order to love the person you are. One of the best ways I know to accomplish this is to release the unresolved pain of childhood. Pain surfaces during break-ups, creating excellent opportunities for us to resolve unresolved pain and become more present to our true nature and life. In the past, I had been unwilling to face the pain. No longer. I was ready, and Chip was ready to teach me how.

Facing the Pain

" When you find yourself obsessing about Christopher, ask yourself, 'What is it about this moment that I don't want to experience right now?'" Chip suggested.

The next time my mind drifted to Christopher, I asked what was so awful about this moment, and I became present. In the present moment, I could see that I was happy.

"Why did you come to me?" Chip asked. I thought a minute. "Because I was in pain?" "But what was it you were seeking?" he probed. "Peace." "Peace, love, joy, awe, energy, the capacity to experience beauty, the innate connection to nature and the cosmos, even your direct experience of the Divine are all expressions of your true nature, or soul. All are available to you, Randy, but you must be present in order to receive them," he said.

"So the pain around my breakup with Christopher is a catalyst for connecting to my true self?" My head felt as if it was going to burst. "Yes, but remember that your wake-up call is always right now in this very moment. That's all you really have. This present moment is your only reality."

He pressed on. "Do you want to savor the drama or be present?" "Both." I had to be honest. It felt good wallowing in my emotions. "You can't serve two masters, my friend," he said. "If you're savoring the drama of the past, you can't be in the present." "What about when something upsetting happens in the present?" I asked. "For example, the dinner party where I saw Christopher. I walked in, spotted Christopher, and in that that moment, I felt as if I had been punched in the belly." "Can you go to that place now?" he coached. I was already there. "What does it feel like?" he asked. "I feel sad." "Good, you're sad. Feel it."

I found myself wanting to change the object of my focus, the subject, or leave the room. I didn't like feeling it. "When you hate a painful feeling, such as sadness, you not only amplify that feeling, you suffer in response to it," he said. "But when you find your own innate capacity for kindness and compassion, you can welcome your painful feelings back into the home of your heart."

"So if I stop hating my sadness and welcome it into my heart, will it then dissipate?" I asked. "It may well dissipate over time because feelings that aren't resisted are free to run their natural course. And that usually involves a natural and organic dissipation." "Good," I said, feeling at least a little reassured. "But if you really stopped hating your sadness and honestly welcomed it into your heart, why would you need it to go away?" he asked. "What are you getting at?" **"Healing is not about getting rid of pain, it's about becoming whole," he explained. "Being whole requires embracing and being at peace with *all* you are, not just the experiences you consider positive. The most direct way to do this is to genuinely welcome those disowned or rejected aspects of your own experience."**

Finding Peace

We continued. I relaxed and entered the feeling again. "What does it feel like?" Chip asked. "I feel sucker punched." "Stick with it," he coached. "Where is it now?" he continued. "It's in my chest. I'm having trouble breathing." "Concentrate on the exhale." I did. "Does the feeling have a shape?" he probed. "Yes, it's round." "Is it solid or soft?" "It's hard." "What size?" he continued. "It's the size of a baseball," I replied. "Where is it now?" "It's now in my shoulder. Wait. It's smaller," I answered. "Stay with it." I did. He continued with his questioning. Soon, the feeling began to dissipate. Was it my imagination or did I relax? Was I feeling peace?

"When we can welcome whatever comes up in the moment without judging it to be good or bad, we connect with our soul. It's then that peace becomes available to us," Chip explained. I remembered reading Victor Frankl's *Man's Search for Meaning* in college. Frankl, a Jew, was deported to the Theresienstadt concentration camp in 1942 where he witnessed unspeakable atrocities. Frankl came to believe that by fully experiencing the suffering objectively, he would thereby end it.

25

Feel First

When you feel intense emotion, welcome it, separate it from story, and sink into sensation," Chip continued. "Ask, 'What am I feeling in my body that I am calling sadness, anger, or whatever?'"
This was not a foreign concept to me. About a year ago, I started taking Pilates and yoga, I explored acupuncture, and I danced—all in an attempt to get more in touch with my emotions. I had been feeling stuck and sensed it was because I hadn't dealt with some sadness and anger that had crept into my life, much of which had to do with my relationship with Christopher. I knew my body harbored emotion, and getting physical would help it move through.

Raphael Cushnir writes in his book, *The One Thing Holding You Back: Unleashing the Power of Emotional Connection*, "Emotions are like weather, constantly passing through the landscape of your physical body." He believes that to experience emotion, we must first develop a keen awareness of physical sensation. He writes, "Feel first, think later." Try to instantly identify the emotion and scan your body for any physical sensation. Like Chip, Cushnir suggests getting microscopic.

Does the sensation move or stay fixed?

Does it change?

Does it have a shape?

Cushnir believes that when we stop and check in with physical sensations, those emotions that require our attention will reveal themselves.

Allow Emotions

Feelings weren't something my family talked about much. I remember the morning my mother woke me with the news that my grandmother had died. I was nine. My first concern was for Dad. "Is he awfully sad?" I asked. I was worried. "He's fine," she said, and that was the last time anyone spoke of my grandmother's death.

My mother died of cancer twenty-two years later. Her death was a slow one. Despite my love for her, I could not grieve. The pain of losing Mother was too intense.

Blocking emotions in one area of my life meant blocking them all. The gurus say that times of great sorrow have the potential to be times of great transformation, but first we must go deep and experience the pain without resistance, judgment, blame, self-pity, or self-identification. In my experience, that's easier said than done. I love what Tom Booker says in the movie, *The Horse Whisperer:* "Sometimes what seems like surrender isn't surrender at all. It's about what's going on in our hearts. About seeing clearly the way life is and accepting it and being true to it, whatever the pain, because the pain of not being true to it is far, far greater."

I am learning there's a difference between, "I am sad," and "I feel sad." When I say, "I am sad," I am identifying with sadness, but when I say, "I feel sad," I put sadness in its proper place. It's an emotion, and like all emotions it will eventually pass.

Stephen Cope, author of *Yoga and the Quest for the True Self,* suggests:

- Breathe
- Relax
- Feel
- Watch
- Allow

And of course, my therapist Chip says to separate feeling from story and sink into sensation.

27

Be Real

I am also learning that being sad, angry—or whatever I may feel— will not destroy my positive image. If anything, it will reinforce my humility and authenticity and create connection. **Sometimes being myself means freeing myself from the image of the way I believe I should be.** I have been over-invested in what I call my "golden boy image," a persona built primarily on being positive and upbeat at all times. Like so many personas, this image is rooted in childhood messages. Mine included:

No one wants to be around a gloomy cuss.
Smile and the whole world smiles with you.
Only weak people wear their emotions on their sleeves.
People will take advantage of you if they see that you are weak.

I've learned that while some may admire my "golden boy image," few can relate to it. Also, I'm now in a stage of life where forging stronger, more intimate relationships is more important than impressing people. When I wallpaper over my sadness and anger to appear positive and upbeat, I am living a lie. I'm not being real. The Skin Horse in *The Velveteen Rabbit* explains, "Generally, by the time you are Real, most of your hair has been loved off, and your eyes drop out and you get loose in your joints and very shabby. But these things don't matter at all, because once you are Real you can't be ugly, except to people who don't understand."

I am learning that living authentically does not mean sharing every possible thought or feeling, but it does mean speaking my truth—even on days when it's not so pretty and positive. I want to be real, not only with others, but with myself. I've experienced loss before—a lot of loss, in fact—but this was the first time that I didn't mask it all. Instead, I leaned into it. But what I still didn't understand was why the breakup packed such a large punch when I wanted it in the first place. I asked Chip about it. "Again, it's not about Christopher," he began.

28

Four Limiting Beliefs

❝ There is almost always a core belief that is central to an emotional wound, and that belief is often what keeps us from healing," he said.

"Four of the most common limiting beliefs are: 'I am not safe'; I am not good'; 'I am not enough'; and, 'I don't belong.' Most of us subscribe to at least one of these." One, okay, but damn! I subscribe to all four.

I am not safe. For me this was the big one. I used to say if I could only be held for a minute and feel all was safe with the world, I would be happy. I obsessed about Christopher during those times that I felt most vulnerable. When Asheville became blanketed in snow and ice, I was a mess. I grew up in Atlanta; Christopher grew up in Connecticut. He was comfortable driving in the snow and ice, and I was not. I didn't know how I was going to survive the winter without him.

I am not good. I would beat myself up that I wasn't over this relationship. I had wanted the breakup. Why couldn't I let go? Worse, why couldn't I forgive him? I must be a bad person.

I am not enough. I found myself thinking, if only I had ___, then ___. Or, if only I were ___, then he'd ___. If only I were more this or that, or I had done that or this, then we'd still be together. If only I was enough.

I don't belong. I came out later in life. I was thirty-nine when I divorced my wife and entered the "gay world." I knew I didn't belong in the heterosexual world, but I was surprised to learn that I didn't fit the gay world either. I now have a sense about what it felt like to be biracial in the 1960s. Most of us long for a tribe.

After leaving our relationship, Christopher became immersed in Asheville's gay scene. He enjoyed an active social life—so active that I had to block him on Facebook. After our breakup, I could no longer stand to see the photographs of Christopher and his friends at parties, hiking, or traveling. Not only was I jealous, it amplified the feeling that I don't belong.

Jealousy, anger, hatred, despair, and loneliness—all those "scary" emotions—are based upon fear, and what are our greatest fears? The four limiting beliefs. None of these beliefs are true. I read once that to become who we are, we have to let go of who we are not. Like so many clever sayings, this is easier said than done.

> **Consider This: Write down any limiting beliefs that may be at work in your life right now.**

29

Letting Go

I t seems to me that society teaches us to hold onto and possess, when it should be teaching us to let go. We'll never live richer, more authentic lives until we do. I had actually written about this concept some years ago for my eNewsletter and had come up with a simple three-step process for letting go of limiting beliefs. I shared it with Chip.

1. Recognize when I am reacting to outdated belief systems. Emotional warning signals include feeling anxious, afraid, indignant, rejected, sorry for myself, ashamed, worried, or confused.

2. Take a deep belly breath and gently observe what I am doing/ feeling without judgment. "Ahhhh, anger (jealousy, or whatever). Oops, there I go again."

3. Examine what has happened and tell myself the truth. For example, when I catch myself worrying about money ("there is not enough"), I remind myself that I have plenty of money on which to live, and I can always make more.

"There's an easier way," Chip suggested. "Would you like to know it?"
"Of course."

"By being present," he answered. "You don't feel safe? Are you safe right this minute?" he asked. "Yes," I replied. "Are you really?" he probed. "Yes." I replied. In that moment, I was feeling safe; I was getting it.

"It's actually quite simple, Randy. Most great truths are. One of life's chief tasks is to awake to the present moment, and at no time are we put more to the test than in relationships. Our reactions to the past contaminate the now. They impact our interpretation of what's taking place. To clear these false beliefs, stop reacting to the past and stop trying to avoid or alter the future. Live in the present."

"Everything seems to come back to being present," I observed. "Now, you're getting it," he said, smiling. Letting go is about freedom, and freedom is about nonattachment. We become comfortable with whatever happens in the moment because we don't have a rigid sense of who we are and what kind of experience or outcome is supposed to happen. In short, we open to the possibilities.

30

Nonattachment

One thought, then another thought. Another one. And another. Following my thoughts taught me about the law of impermanence, or what the Buddhists call "nonattachment." This is a tough lesson for me to absorb; I find safety in the illusion of permanence.

Growing up, a group of mothers took turns carpooling us kids to and from school. Sometimes, the mothers would stop on the way home at Barfield's, an Atlanta "five and dime" with a large candy selection. Most mothers would give us a dime (my mother grudgingly doled out a nickel). While the other children purchased a candy bar or two, I looked for something more permanent, perhaps a small toy or trinket. A candy bar was fleeting, but a toy! You could hold on to that.

As an adult, I'm far more interested in learning how to let go rather than hold on. I'd like to practice nonattachment and allow people, places, situations, and things to flow through me. I already have a precedent for this in my life—my art collection. For more than thirty years, I've collected Southern folk art. At one time, I possessed more than three hundred pieces.

Over the years, I've sold or given away hundreds of pieces from my collection. It's fun to see where some of them have landed. Some of the stronger ones hang in museums, others are in galleries or private collections, and a few are featured in beautiful coffee table books. It's fun to attend a museum exhibition or pick up a book and see a piece that was once mine. It's strange, but it also feels right. I'm learning that while I may purchase a piece of art, I am never its owner. I'm only a steward. If only I could do the same with people. It took almost as long as we were married for me to let go of my ex-wife.

A spiritual teacher once explained that I "corded" to people. Cording is a metaphysical term that describes a type of energetic communication between two or more people. Cords are created with thoughts, and thoughts create energetic links. If the thought is casual or occurs infrequently, it's a temporary connection and will dissolve over time. But if it's frequent, obsessive, or emotionally charged, it can become permanent. This type of cord is like an emotional umbilical cord; but unlike an umbilical cord that is cut at birth, cords remain in place until they are removed.

31

Cutting the Cord

I went online to learn how to remove cords and found several sites offering different strategies. One suggested going to a trained energy healer. Another suggested the "golden hula hoop," an envisioning process: one sets a clear intention of removing all the cords, then passes an imaginary gold hoop down the entire length of his or her body while visualizing the hoop severing all unhealthy connections. My favorite strategy was to visualize where the cords enter the body, then to gently pull each as if it were a weed, careful to ensure that all the roots were removed. Once pulled, I visualized sending the cords back to their source and calling my energy to return and repair the wounds. Cords are persistent, the sites explained. These processes might have to be done daily and several times a day.

While I didn't tell many people, I tried all three strategies. I went to an energy worker who shook a rattle over my body to clear my chakras and cut the cords. I visualized the golden hula hoop, as well as pulling the cords as if they were weeds. I also prayed.

A friend who had been through a difficult breakup sent me a wonderful prayer by Marianne Williamson. I changed the first line and deleted the second. My new prayer read:

Dear God,
I am bonded in heart to someone who no longer serves my best interest.
Please, dear God, disconnect my heart from this
longing within me that does not serve.
I release this person into Your hands.
May the ropes that bind my heart be cut.
May they not bind me.
May they not bind him.
I release him that I might be released.
Retract the silent hooks I have sent him.
Bring back the power and my love.
Cut the cord that chemically ties me to him.
Free me from him.
Free him from me.
May we find peace.
Free us both.
Amen

My friend Carla liked the idea of adapting an existing prayer so much that she adapted one herself. She found a prayer on death and changed the words so that they were applicable to her divorce.

Mantras help too. A mantra is a sound, syllable, word, or group of words that are considered capable of "creating transformation." I wrote one and repeated it often. It read:

The karmic debt has been paid.
The bonds are broken.
I release you in love and light.
I now welcome this new moment.

While all of these tactics were helpful in managing sadness, none was more effective than shattering the illusion and embracing the truth.

32

Shatter the Illusion

O ne of my favorite writers is Pearl S. Buck. Pearl knew a thing or two about broken hearts. She once wrote, "There were many ways of breaking a heart. Stories were full of hearts broken by love, but what really broke a heart was taking away its dream—whatever that dream might be."

When Dad died, mother turned him into a saint. My father was a good man, but he was no saint. Widows—and some widowers—do this often, I am told. And similarly to those grieving the loss of a spouse, those of us dealing with a painful breakup may be tempted to reinvent history. Memories of the relationship and our ex-partners can become distorted.

"I found peace once I realized that what I cried about the most had never been real," my friend Lynn shared. She continued. "I was missing an idealized version of my boyfriend, and the hopes, dreams, and plans for the future that I mourned were only fantasies, mere stories that I had made up in my imagination. Once I accepted that fact, I could move on." Whenever I felt sad about my breakup, I tried to remember Lynn's excellent advice. It wasn't the real Christopher that I missed as much as the illusion I had created for Christopher and our relationship.

33

Get On With It

Ten months after our breakup, I ran into Christopher at the grocery store. My heart stopped. Asheville is a small town, but somehow we had never run into one another. He saw me first. Neither of us spoke. That didn't feel right. As I rolled my buggy past him, I nervously called out, "Hey, Christopher." Looking straight ahead, he didn't return my greeting. I took no offense. He was doing the best he could. We both were.

Still, our exchange upset me. Shouldn't we be further along with the process? Author Barbara DeAngelis seemed to think so. In her book *How to Make Love All the Time*, DeAngelis identifies the four stages of a breakup.

Stage One: The Tearing Apart
Two weeks to two months
In it, you feel lost, alone, and sorry for yourself. You remember and cry a lot. You are tempted to return to your ex-partner.

Stage Two: The Adjustment
Two to six months
You begin to re-form (or reclaim) your personality and identity. You have a clearer idea of what went wrong and no longer feel like a victim. You can think about or talk to your ex-partner without becoming angry or feeling like you'll fall apart. You begin making plans for the future.

Stage Three: Healing
Six months to one year
You no longer feel you are in transition. You are in or are interested in a new relationship. You can talk to your partner without becoming immediately upset. You feel sad or nostalgic less often—maybe once a week or every two weeks.

Stage Four: Recovery
One to two years
You no longer think of yourself as having just ended a relationship. You have learned the lessons and adopted new ways of being as a result of what you've learned. You are happy in your new life.

Our grocery store encounter suggested that I was stuck in stage two, the adjustment phase. Still, I reminded myself that I was making progress. While I was unsettled, I wasn't as upset as I would have been a month earlier. And shortly after the encounter when I started to obsess, I remembered the call to become present. Maybe it wouldn't be much longer before I'd be able to forgive him and myself, release us, and move on.

There is no set way to let go. There's no particular process, no right or wrong way, and no set time frame. Everyone's experience is his own. Above all, it's imperative to respect the process, find compassion for yourself and your ex-partner, and know that if you can stay aware and awake, there are valuable lessons to be learned that will help you grow and enrich your life.

34

Forgiving, Forgiveness

I never understood why my ex-wife didn't want to be friends until after I experienced the breakup with Christopher. Now the shoe was on the other foot. Christopher wanted to be friends, and I didn't. I suspected what Christopher really wanted was absolution in the same way I wanted absolution from my ex-wife. "Absolution is not mine to give," I told a friend. (My angry words would come back to bite me.)

I now understood my ex-wife's perspective, and for the first time since our divorce, I could let go. I was able to let go in the same way I wanted Christopher to let go of me. It wouldn't be long before the Universe put me to the test—less than a month later I saw my ex-wife at our goddaughter's wedding. "She's actually looking forward to seeing you," my goddaughter's mother and dear friend told me. I tried not to build any expectations around our reunion. Despite my friend's words, I knew it could go either way.

My ex was polite but frosty. I felt sad and disappointed, but her attitude didn't carry the charge it once did. If I wanted forgiveness, I would have to forgive myself. After all, absolution was not hers to give. When I was ready to forgive myself, I could finally stop looking for another person to make me feel better about myself.

As difficult as it would be forgiving Christopher, it would be a lot easier than forgiving myself. Rationally, I knew that Christopher and I had done the best we could at the time. Still, I wasn't ready to forgive either of us. The Aramaic word for "forgive" is to "untie." I wanted to untie and move on. Or did I? In truth, I wasn't ready to sever the emotional cord that bound us, the invisible hooks I had sunk into him.

At the same time, I didn't like the person I had become. I wanted to be in a place where I wished Christopher all the good things I want in my own life. At times, I did find compassion and I sent him a blessing. But more often than not, I wanted him to feel that the biggest mistake he made in his life was giving me up.

Whether I was angry with myself or someone else, the most direct route to forgiveness was to separate from the story, drop below the blame to where the deeper pain lies, sink into sensation, and allow my inner life to be what it was. I remembered Chip's words, "Be where you are." Forgiveness was not where I was in that moment. Eventually I'd forgive, but trying to force it only delays its coming. The best I could do was to intend to one day forgive Christopher.

35

Lessons Learned About Waking Up

- All great teachers agree that peace, wisdom, joy, and awe are already within you, but to receive them you must be present.

- At any given moment ask yourself these two questions: "Where is the focus of my attention?" and "What is the intensity, or depth, of my attention?" In these two questions lies the key for waking up and becoming present.

- When you catch yourself in a fantasy, obsession, plan, or memory, ask yourself: "Why am I trying to escape this present moment?"

- Focus on the "what is" rather than "what if." Guard against fantasies, especially idealized versions of your ex-partner and your relationship together.

- Almost everyone I talked with agreed: short-term pain equals long-term gain. When you feel intense emotion, welcome it, separate it from the story, and sink into sensation.

- Relationships give an excellent opportunity to identify and work through limiting beliefs. Ask yourself which false beliefs are being activated: I don't belong; I'm not good; I'm not enough; and I am not safe. See them as wake-up calls to be present. Are you safe in this moment? Good? Enough? Belong? And so on.

- Remember the law of impermanence. This will pass. Everything does.

- Forgiving—yourself and your ex-partner—is an important element of letting go. That said, you cannot manufacture forgiveness, but you can remain open to it. With intention, forgiveness will most likely come in time.

Part Four

Breakthrough

When you don't pay attention, you're forced to repeat the class. The same is true for relationships. When you don't learn the lessons from a failed relationship, you are likely to repeat them, and you'll end up dating someone with the same issues that worked your last nerve the last time.

Learning the lessons requires compassion for yourself and your ex-partner. It means putting blame aside and taking personal responsibility. Regardless of what happened in the relationship, know that you had a role to play. My friend David knows. When I asked him how he survived his breakup, he told me, "Deep, no-holds-barred self-examination. For example, if I attract someone who is selfish and self-centered, I have to be willing to heal that hidden place in me that attracted that experience."

Doing your homework helps you heal and move on. Once you acknowledge the lessons you've learned, you can reclaim the gifts the relationship brought you, rather than feeling the relationship was a mistake. Taking time for introspection is imperative if you want to deepen your ability to love and be loved, and it's absolutely mandatory if you want to make your intimate relationship a part of your spiritual practice. Relationships become spiritual practice when they serve as vehicles to discover our true self, essence, or what many call "our divine self."

36

The Pause

After my rebound relationship with Thomas, I swore off dating—and sex—for three months. My friends didn't think celibacy would last. "Celibate summer? You'll be lucky to make it through Saturday," they teased. Celibate summer wasn't as hard as I (or they) thought. In fact, I enjoyed it. I loved spending time with friends, as well as having time to embrace my new-found singleness.

When fall arrived, I didn't rush into dating. The last thing I wanted to do was embark on another "manic manhunt." Instead, I continued to spend time with friends and with myself. In his book *Transitions: Making Sense of Life's Changes*, William Bridgers observed that people in transition seem to almost always find time for being alone and away from familiar distractions. I called this time "the pause."

Pauses come after those pivotal times when life brings us to our knees. A pause could be due to a loss of job, direction, or a relationship. Pauses are "desert time," opportunities that allow us to sink into silence, stillness, reflection, and introspection. Spiritual writer Marianne Williamson refers to the pause as "tomb time," the time between crucifixion and resurrection. Bridgers calls this time of "inner reorientation" the "neutral-zone," when one experiences emptiness "in which the old reality looks transparent and nothing feels solid anymore." During the pause, life as we know it shifts. For me, work slowed down, I wasn't motivated to write or paint, and I couldn't even concentrate enough to read.

Bridgers says not to fight it. "The first of the neutral-zone activities or functions is surrender—the person must give in to the emptiness and stop struggling to escape it."

One of my dear friends, Kathy, experienced the pause around the same time I did. She said she was "sitting on the park bench with Eckhart." Eckhart is Eckhart Tolle, author of *The Power of Now: A Guide to Spiritual Enlightenment* and *A New Earth: Awakening to Your Life's Purpose*. Kathy was practicing Tolle's call to be present. **"I am accepting 'what is' and embracing 'whatever,'"** she explained. "Most times I have good days, but every now and then I have a not-so-good day. The not-so-good ones happen when I project from the present to the future and collapse into fear."

Kathy was a wonderful guide. She wasn't sure where life was leading her, but she trusted that Divine Order was at play. Sitting peacefully in the pause, she believed that a path—the right path—would eventually open up. For now, her only job was to stay awake, observe, and listen for the lessons.

37

Ask Yourself

A s difficult as a breakup is, it can also be a transformative experience. Bernie Siegel (no relation) once wrote: "Life is a labor pain; we are here to give birth to ourself."

The pause is the perfect time to examine what attracted us to our ex, what worked in the relationship, what didn't work in the relationship, and what we'd like to take forward or drop.

Journaling was my salvation. In addition to helping me get through this breakup, it:

- allowed me to deal with my issues honestly in the privacy of my journal.
- brought clarity to many challenges while providing an outlet for pent-up emotions.
- provided an outlet for pent-up emotions.
- documented insights.
- gave my dreams and ideas a place to grow.
- charted my process and progress.

If you've never journaled before, don't be intimidated. It's easy. Purchase a fun notebook, diary, or journal, and get a good pen. Or write on your computer. What's important is that you write freely and honestly.

Don't worry about grammar or spelling. Keep it private. Your journal is for you and you alone.

When I journaled, I used a variety of tools such as list making, dialoging, and letter writing. I made lists of lessons learned, things that I was grateful for from the relationship, and reasons why I was angry. Sometimes I wrote a dialog between me and an aspect of myself, such as Sad Self and Higher Self. Or I would write a dialog between me and Christopher on an issue that needed resolution. These dialogs helped me get a clearer understanding of both his and my perspectives on particular issues. I also wrote Christopher several letters that I never mailed.

Another easy approach to journaling is to ask yourself a question. I have found these twelve questions particularly inspiring:

1. Why did I attract my ex into my life? (We tend to attract, or be drawn to, people that reflect how we feel about ourselves, our lives, love, and relationships.)

2. Why was he/she the right person at the time? (This question was especially powerful for me. In answering it, I realized that Christopher was the perfect person at the perfect time for several reasons. First, he was the first person I lived with after my divorce. Moving in with someone was stressful, but Christopher made it easy. He moved into my house and life gently, with little disruption. Additionally, I had recently entered my fifties and was feeling my age. Christopher was much younger than me. With Christopher on my arm, I felt young and attractive.)

3. What worked well in the relationship and what didn't?

4. What would I do differently next time?

5. How was this relationship similar to past relationships? Am I following a pattern? And if so, is this a pattern I want to continue or break?

6. Which of the four limiting beliefs were activated during the relationship? How about during the breakup? What activated them?

7. What was it I wanted most from my partner that I didn't receive or get enough of? Was it something I could have provided for myself?

8. What was I most proud of about our relationship? What brought me the most shame?

9. What new habits did I develop in the relationship? Which do I want to keep or let go?

10. What disowned traits did I project onto my ex-partner? (We tend to be attracted to people who have traits that we also possess but have disowned. For example, I used to be attracted to creative men until I finally claimed my own creativity.)

11. How did I exit the relationship? In what ways did I avoid time and intimacy with my partner? (Some might include work, watching television, playing computer games, or reading novels.)

12. Was there a central lesson? If so, what was it?

As you can see from the above questions, one of the keys to learning the lessons is reviewing past relationships. Even if you think you've already done this, do it again. With each new relationship, you are better able to understand the past.

> **Consider This: For the next twelve days, pick a different question and journal about it.**

38

Learning from the Past

We attract partners who mimic the wounds we received from our parents in the hope that our partner will help heal our past. My father was distant, and my mother was emotionally needy. In response, I've chosen some partners who were withdrawn and others who clung. I clung to those who withdrew and distanced myself from those who tried to fuse with me.

We also attract partners who possess strengths and skills we feel we lack. Breaking up—or being in a conscious relationship—presents an opportunity to reclaim these strengths and abilities for ourselves.

I mentioned earlier that I had many fears around safety after Christopher left, and one of them was driving in the snow. The winter after Christopher and I split was a harsh one, and I had to learn to drive in the snow. While I am still somewhat fearful, I can do it—and with each snowfall, my confidence increases.

We also project our negative traits onto our partners. I've learned to pay particular attention when I criticize a partner for something he has done; inevitably it's something I do myself. For example, I wished that Christopher was neater, yet I used to throw my dirty gym clothes on the bedroom chair.

> **Consider This: Write down three complaints that you often had about your ex. Is it possible that you also do the same things?**

39

Other Lessons Learned

Glance at my bookshelves and you'll see a slew of self-help books on relationships. And I've lost count of all the workshops I've attended. I've tried to practice much of what I've learned, but much of it is formulaic, and most times I can't remember the formula. What I do remember comes from direct experience. Here's a sampling of what I took forward with me from my breakup.

Commitment

Commitment is a tricky one for me. On one hand, I feel a relationship is doomed unless both partners commit to riding out the bad times as well as enjoying the good. Relationships aren't always easy. Problems arise. The secret to longevity is to embrace these problems as opportunities for growth—and not bolt! On the other hand, I am not convinced that everyone can truly commit to "until death do us part." I believe the best we can do is commit to an intention to stay with our partners until we believe we've learned all we came into the relationship to learn.

This I do know: I don't want to enter into another intimate relationship without being fully committed. I couldn't commit fully to the relationship with Christopher because I didn't trust that he'd be there for me in my old age. When he would be my age now, I'd be in my seventies. I couldn't fathom he'd want to stick around. In retrospect, I shouldn't have made assumptions about Christopher's commitment. I should have shared my fears and perhaps my honesty and vulnerability would have brought us closer.

Consciousness

We humans love mirrors, and there are few mirrors better than relationships. Like the Velveteen Rabbit learned, in order to feel real, we must feel seen, heard, understood, accepted, and loved. Psychologists call this a narcissistic need for mirroring. Yet psychologists also tell us we have a tendency to look in the mirror and see what is not really true. **Instead of reality, we see a distorted image based upon our perceptions of the past.** Conscious relationships have the potential to help us see ourselves and our lives as they really are.

Chip liked to say great relationships are built on what he calls "radical intimacy." Radical intimacy can only occur when we place our stories aside and sink into the present moment. This means that the person I reveal to you is the same person I am discovering I am in this moment. Or in Chip's words, "The discovery of who I am in this moment is one and the same as the revealing of who I am. It's as if we say to the other, 'I reserve the right not to be who either of us thinks I am.'"

Curiosity

One of the most important ingredients in a successful relationship is curiosity. **A relationship dies the moment we begin to believe that we know all there is to know about the other person. Such an assumption is preposterous, anyway, since we're always changing from one moment to the next.**

Curiosity helps us stay engaged in the relationship; it helps us stay present. I loved it when Christopher asked me about my painting, and Christopher loved it when I asked him about his music collection. For a very short while, I shared pieces of art that I loved with Christopher, he likewise shared music that he particularly loved with me. How much stronger our relationship would have been if we had continued that practice.

Honesty

Above all, I want to be seen, heard, and understood, but I can't be seen, heard, or understood until I allow others to see, hear, and understand all my thoughts and feelings in the moment. Barbara DeAngelis writes that there's a big difference between the complete truth and being honest.

I can be totally honest with my friends, but it's much harder with my significant other. I fear that he may judge, ridicule, or worse, leave me. Yet seldom has this been the case. What I've found is that the more I share—even when the sharing is uncomfortable—the closer we become.

Communications

I found personality typing tools, especially the Myers-Briggs Personality Index and the Enneagram, to be especially helpful in helping me understand and better communicate with my partners. Myers-Briggs taught me *how* Christopher communicated, and the Enneagram explained *why* he communicated the way he did. I also found the work of Dr. Gary Chapman helpful. According to Chapman, there are five ways to express and seek love:

One: Words of Affirmation

Two: Gifts

Three: Acts of Service

Four: Quality Time

Five: Physical Touch

One of the ways I feel loved is through gifts. It's not the physical gift that's important to me—it's the expression of love behind it. Growing up, my father often gave me gifts that were educational. Because I felt there was an agenda attached to these gifts, they seldom brought me joy. I love fresh flowers. When Christopher brought me a bouquet, I was elated. Christopher experienced love through quality time. When I took the time to listen intently or initiate an intimate or intellectual conversation, he felt loved.

Neither of us was proficient in the other's love language. Instead of whining that my needs weren't being met, I learned to ask for what I want. I once asked him to plan, organize, and implement a "date night." He rose to the occasion: flowers, a nice dinner, and the theater. I felt wonderful!

Sex is another way to communicate in relationships. In a conscious relationship, it's hard—if not impossible—to separate sex from intimacy. Like many men, I know a good bit about sex, but I have much to learn about intimacy.

Sex and Intimacy

I once read a fascinating article on sex and love in *Psychology Today*. In it, writer Elizabeth Devita-Raeburn observed, "Sex, and more importantly, intimacy, are grown-up skills, and most of us, metaphorically speaking, are still in junior high." As much as I hate to admit it, I can relate. Technically, I'd like to think that I'm at least on college level, but sex is not engineering—or as one of my friends likes to say, "performance sex."

Great sex requires more than technique; great sex is connected sex. Sex is a language, and its vocabulary reflects everything that is happening in the relationship.

For Christopher and me, the quality of our sex life fluctuated depending on where we were emotionally in our relationship. The best sex we enjoyed was during those weeks between the time we decided to separate and when Christopher left. I believe this was because we were both so vulnerable.

In the *Psychology Today* article, sex therapist David Schnarch said that great sex is inherently based upon intimacy, and most of us don't have a clue what real intimacy is all about. We look to our partners to make us feel good and validate us—to make us whole—but few relationships can survive that. And according to Schnarch, few should. "Ultimately, you get through gridlock and get to a place of more honest self-disclosure, where the focus is on being known, rather than being validated." Put another way, **intimacy equals "into me see."** When sexuality and intimacy are in partnership, they can become a centerpiece for personal development, and that's what I wanted for my next relationship.

Codependence

My friend Robert shared: "I learned that while compromise is necessary, making sure that I don't lose myself is more important. I've seen a pattern in my last two major relationships where I lost track of me, while trying to please my other half." Caroline, another friend, chimed in: "It took me almost a lifetime to learn, understand, and accept where I stop and others begin. Breakups have been the best teachers."

After my split with Christopher, I examined how I lost myself in relationships. When I was not anchored, I got swept away by another's emotions, opinions, or moods. I lost my power. I learned that when I lost my power, I short circuited any chance of a meaningful relationship. I became resentful. These power outages generated anger—mostly with myself.

I read once that when you give up yourself to a relationship, your partner has no choice but to leave you. It's just too much pressure for him or her to have to be the missing piece that makes you whole. This tracks with my experience. Right before my ex-wife and I separated, I said to her, "I'm having a hard enough time living my own life, I can't live yours for you too." While this was not one of my more compassionate moments, it was true.

I wanted a relationship of equals, but too often I shrunk in order to make the relationship work. I was scared of being abandoned. Not in touch with my true self, I lost my footing. I became untethered. My anchor broke and I drifted out to sea. When I became more aware, confident, and content with all that I am, I began to recognize that "I am enough." I found dry land.

I'm realizing the value of these lessons in other relationships as well. After ending a recent phone conversation with a friend, I was exhausted. Like a psychic leech, she drained every bit of energy I had. I am learning not to blame, however, but to examine. Accepting responsibility, I asked myself, "What am I here to learn?" I saw that once again I was losing my power. Playing her parent, I had tried to fix her brokenness. I had given advice when she had asked for none. The next time we talked, I just listened. This time, I did not make her problems my own, and at the end of our conversation, I didn't feel drained.

I made this pledge to myself:

I will retain my power; I will be aware when, like acid, fear bubbles forth.

I will address concerns despite my fears of abandonment and conflict.

I will not become the parent, or worse, play the role of a child.

I will remember that intimacy starts with sharing self, yet I will stop giving so much I resent it.

I will allow others to give to me in return.

But most of all, I will stay true to self and my values. I will remember that **all love begins with loving me.**

> **Consider This: Write down three to seven lessons you've learned that you'd like to take with you into your next relationship.**

40

The Central Lesson

❝ Have you learned the central lesson?" my friend asked, placing her hand over my heart. I answered honestly, "I'm not sure." Her question stuck with me, and for the next few weeks I continued to ask myself what central lesson I had learned from my split with Christopher. "Knowing you, you'll come up with three bullets all beginning with the letter *c*," another friend who knew me well teased.

Then one day it hit me: the greatest gift I received during my breakup was awakening to my divinity. **My breakup taught me how to become more present, and when I become present, I connect to "Presence," or God. When I connect to "Presence," I'm aware that love, joy, peace, awe—all the gifts of God—are available to me all the time *in this moment*.**

Eckhart Tolle writes in *A New Earth: Awakening to Your Life's Purpose*, "Some Christian mystics have called it Christ within; Buddhists call it your Buddha nature; for Hindus, it's Atman, the indwelling God. When you are in touch with that dimension within yourself—and being in touch with it is your natural state, not some miraculous achievement—all your actions and relationships will reflect the oneness with all life that you sense deep within. This is love."

When I felt disconnected, Chip suggested I ask myself: "What am I doing at this moment that is giving me the false impression that I'm not in the belly of the Divine?" What a beautiful image, and what a powerful question! More importantly, what a wonderful way to live!

41

Lessons Learned About Breaking Through

- Find a regular time and place to be alone. Be gentle with yourself. Now might not be a good time for intense activity. Surrender into "The Pause."

- Now is a good time to review past relationships and decide what you'd like to start, stop, or continue in your next relationship.

- Great relationships require commitment, consciousness, curiosity, radical honesty, strong communications, and a connection between sex and intimacy. It's also important to guard against codependency.

- Breakups are a great time to learn about becoming more present. When this happens, you are in the presence of the Divine. Put another way, a breakup—like any major life transition—offers an excellent opportunity to connect with your divinity.

- When we connect to our divinity, love, joy, peace, awe—all the gifts of God—are immediately available to us.

I'm proud that I took time for introspection, and am grateful for the lessons I learned. As I became more conscious of all that had happened during and after the relationship, I became more grateful for the time spent with Christopher. I saw how our relationship was a precious gift.

Letting go and learning the lessons take time—sometimes a lot of time. However, you don't have to wait until you've *totally* let go or have learned *all* your lessons in order to move on.

Part Five

Move On

What percentage of time you spend on letting go, learning the lessons, and moving on depends on where you are in your process. At the beginning of my split with Christopher, I devoted more time to letting go. Later, learning the lessons received the majority of my attention. After that, I was able to focus on moving on. I became less obsessed with the past, more focused on the present, and increasingly optimistic about the future. Moving on is a time to realign with your values and interests, and to visualize the life and partner you hope to attract.

42

Clean House

I t's been said that if you're unhappy, smile and your emotions will follow. Sometimes taking even the smallest actions can help move the heart into a new direction. I guess that's why rituals work as well as they do. One of the first steps of moving on is to clean house—both physically and metaphorically. Rid your house of reminders. Also, take a close look at aspects of your life acquired while you were together, including friendships, diet, activities, and habits. I'll get into this in more detail later.

Soon after Christopher left, I threw out or packed up all of the things that reminded me of the relationship, including framed photographs, gifts, and souvenirs from trips taken together. Months later, I found a box in the basement filled with his photo albums and college papers. I packed it up and left it with a mutual friend.

Christopher's office remained empty for months after he left. My buddy Jonathan, an interior decorator, finally said to me, "Randy, you've got to do something about this empty room. It's beginning to feel like a mausoleum." Jonathan was right. That week, I moved my painting studio into Christopher's former office.

Articles on breaking up advise us to clean house, reorganize, and redecorate. My friend Melinda found "pillow therapy" especially helpful. She told me, "I placed new decorative pillows on my sofa, chairs, and bed. It was an inexpensive way to change the look of my house." Redecorating helped another friend cope. "I completely changed my bedroom. New paint, carpet, and a new bed. I went from a traditional look to a Zen one. I started sleeping better and the mornings were much happier. As an added bonus, I gave my old furniture to my housekeeper. She was thrilled. It was a win-win situation."

I found other ways to clean house. "Bob" and "Betty" were friends of both Christopher and me, though they were closer with him. We had spent a lot of time with them, but they really never fed my soul. Since Christopher and I broke up, Bob and Betty had called several times to get together. While I truly appreciated their calls, I just didn't want to continue the friendship. We didn't have much in common, and to be honest I found them a little dull. Each time they called, I begged off saying that I had plans. In time, they quit calling. Perhaps there was a more direct way to handle this, but this was the kindest way I knew.

Finally, I looked at the daily activities or habits I had incorporated while in my relationship and noted the compromises I had made. I poured a half-full carton of soy milk down the sink, swore off scary or dark television shows or movies, and started going to bed earlier. Melinda also looked at the compromises she made in her former relationship. Here's a poem she wrote about one of them:

Red Toenail Polish
Painting my toes red.
Sexy. Flirty. Fun.
But you never liked it.
Flashy. Trashy. Inappropriate.

You wanted my toes clear.
Boring. Natural. Plain.
I chose very light silver.
Bland. With a sparkle.

For years, no red on my toes.
Okay. Compromise. Fair.
Now you have left me.
Sad. Shocked. Bereft.

And I'm painting my toes red.

Whenever I see Melinda's bright red toenail polish, I smile. In the subtlest of ways, Melinda has reclaimed her power and given her ex a brightly manicured finger.

> **Consider This: Review the friends, diet, activities, and habits you picked up during your relationship and list no more than five things, if any, that you'd like to change.**

43

Surviving Holidays

olidays can be a bitch after a breakup. Every holiday becomes
"the first..." without your ex. Ginger remembered her first
Fourth of July without her boyfriend. She was walking in her
neighborhood, smelling her neighbors' cookouts, and becoming despondent. "We used to cook out every Fourth," she explained.

Strategies for dealing with the sadness during holidays vary. When
my first Christmas without Christopher rolled around, I maintained my
familiar traditions, such as putting up a tree. When I found ornaments
that we had bought together on trips, I became sad. I kept the ornaments,
but left them in the box that year. When subsequent special occasions
came up, I decided to shake things up. To celebrate one birthday after the
breakup, I took a trip. On another, I planned my own surprise party.

I asked my friend Melinda how she survived the holidays after her
particularly painful breakup. "I tried to remind myself that it's only
twenty-four hours, just like every other day," she said. Another friend got
creative. "As a child-free woman, Mother's Day was particularly hard for
me after my breakup. I decided to make the most of it by sending cards
to friends who viewed their pets as children. I was amazed at the positive
response to my modest outreach. I felt great all day."

44

Exes as Friends?

F orgiveness was one thing, but would I—could I—did I even want to—become friends with Christopher? I asked friends what they thought. Most agreed that it is rare when you can remain friends with your ex. Claire had a different perspective: "Staying friends was always important to me but in retrospect that might be a weird self-preservation thing. My friends always thought I was crazy." Even Claire agreed that staying friends with an ex was tough stuff. Jealousy, sexual chemistry, anger, and hurt can hinder true friendships.

In the past, I had never remained friends with an ex, with one exception—a woman I had dated some years ago. She and I had two factors working for us: first, we didn't have contact for three years after our relationship, and second, we had been close friends before we became romantic.

Research proves the importance of being friends before becoming romantic. In a 1989 study, Metts, Cupach, and Bejlovec found that being friends prior to romantic involvement was a significant predictor of maintaining a friendship after a breakup. Could Christopher and I become friends? At first, I didn't think so, but that was before "Loodle the Poodle."

Loodle came into my life after I lost Lucy, my beloved fourteen-year old Dalmatian. Lucy died only a year after Christopher and I had split, and I had never felt so alone. "Loodle the Poodle" helped me heal, and brought me much joy. My heart was so full it felt like it would burst! Puppies have a way opening even the most closed of hearts.

I was on my way home from taking Loodle to her first veterinarian's appointment when I passed the neighborhood coffee shop. Glancing over at the parking lot, I saw *his* car. As if on autopilot, my car pulled into the lot and before I knew it I was standing in front of Christopher with Loodle in my arms. "Meet Loodle," I began…

A week later, Christopher and I met for a glass of wine. After exchanging preliminary pleasantries, I placed a painted plastic soldier on the table and declared, "I'm through fighting this; I surrender. Whatever our relationship is meant to be, it will be." Christopher shared that he had been equally haunted by our breakup. Had we made a mistake? Should we give the relationship another chance? Neither of us knew, and we were okay with not knowing. Over the next few months, we continued to talk, and over time it became evident that we were meant to be friends, not lovers. I now consider Christopher one of my best buddies.

45

Ideal Relationship Profile

Before I met Christopher, I completed an exercise that promised to be a good way to manifest the man I was seeking—I wrote an ideal partner description. I had high hopes it would guide me in a good direction, but found it really wasn't that helpful. I could list every attribute I wanted, but in the end chemistry trumps any attribute. Additionally, I know now that **the ideal partner is the person who will lead me back to a more authentic relationship with myself.**

So after Christopher, instead of an ideal partner profile, I wrote an ideal *relationship* profile. It included:

1. We have fun together.
2. We are supportive of each other; we are each other's biggest cheerleader.
3. We communicate well. We listen intently to one another. We aren't afraid to talk about the tough stuff.
4. We have a sense of adventure and exploration. We are careful not to fall into a rut.
5. We travel well together.
6. We share several mutual goals.
7. We share household tasks.
8. We have good connected sex.
9. We share similar interests but bring new interests to the relationship.

10. We are considerate of one another.

11. We do not take each other for granted.

12. We are financially independent.

13. We have a good sense of humor and can laugh at ourselves.

14. We take responsibility for our actions.

15. We spend time together but give each other the space the other needs.

16. We share a commitment to self-awareness and development.

17. We are committed to a healthy lifestyle (food and exercise).

18. We are monogamous.

19. We love animals.

20. We are generous.

I then broke down this list into ten "preferences" (notice that I didn't say "needs").

1. Chemistry: I want to find him—and hope he'll find me—attractive. I want us to delight in each other's presence.

2. Commonality: I want to share similar values, interests, lifestyles, and dreams. This was perhaps the biggest tripping point for Christopher and me. Opposites may attract each other, but I'm not convinced they have the staying power to forge a long-term relationship. I want to attract a man who believes as I do that relationships can be a spiritual practice.

3. Respect: I want to respect him, and I want him to respect me. I want us to be proud of one another. I've found that if I don't respect my partner but stay in the relationship anyway, I'll eventually lose respect for myself.

4. Support: We must help each other be his best by being each other's comforter and confronter. I want to be my partner's head cheerleader, and I want to focus on his good attributes, instead of what I'd like to change. At the same time, I want my partner to be open to having me call him down on his junk and invite him to call me down on mine.

5. Communication: I want to be willing to share my life from what I did today to my deepest secrets. I want to build what I call a "safe container" where we both feel safe enough to commit to fully "showing up."

6. Commitment: I want to be committed to doing the work even when it gets hard. I want to remember that working through the tough stuff makes us closer and helps us grow.

7. Aware: I want to be clear on what is mine, his, and ours. I want to take responsibility for my actions when they are less than noble. When I criticize, I want to be aware that I am most likely criticizing an aspect of myself that I don't admire.

8. Awake: I want to be present to my thoughts and emotions. I don't want to create a story or false image of who my partner is. I don't want to react based upon false beliefs or hurts from my past.

9. Engagement: I want to guard against withdrawing. I don't want to disappear from the relationship in television, the Internet, or work.

10. Fun: I want to laugh often, explore the world, share friends, and enjoy life.

Consider This: Write what you'd like in an ideal relationship, then list your top ten "preferences."

46

Dating Again

One of the best pieces of advice I can offer you after a breakup is to postpone dating until you're truly over your ex. I know first-hand: rebound relationships rarely last, and while they provide a nice distraction, they also delay the healing process.

Before dating, ask yourself if you're genuinely interested in going out or if you're just trying to distract yourself to lessen the pain. To answer this question effectively, you have to be completely honest about your emotions and motivations. Then when you're out on the date, pay attention and notice if you're constantly comparing your date to your ex. If you are, you're probably not ready to date. "That's really good advice, Randy," a friend shared. "For a long time after my breakup, I spent most of every date comparing the guy I was with to my ex. Those poor guys! They never had a chance, and I must have been an awful date. Talk about baggage! I was so loaded down, I needed a porter to help me carry it all."

Perhaps the best advice on dating after a breakup comes from a friend who is a counselor. She advises clients not to start dating until they've ranked how much they love themselves on a scale from one to ten, with one being "not at all" and ten being "totally and completely." If the score is less than seven, she recommends delaying dating. She believes— and I agree—there's no recommended amount of time to wait between relationships; the best indicator for relationship readiness is how you feel about yourself.

47

Completion

While I was in the thick of my breakup, I listed several markers that would let me know that I had moved on:

1. I no longer checked my e-mail constantly hoping for a message from him.

2. I stopped looking for him in places that I knew he frequent.

3. I stopped pricking my ears when I heard his name mentioned. More importantly, I stopped reacting physically, like getting that sick feeling in my stomach, when I ran into him.

4. I totally forgave him and me. I genuinely hoped that good things would come his way.

5. I thought of Christopher as a friend—or the man I once dated—rather than my ex.

6. Above all, I felt grateful for our time together.

I learned the last one from my girlfriend Penelope. She e-mailed me this advice: "I used to be furious with my ex, but several weeks ago I had an epiphany. It hit me how wonderful my life has been since our divorce. My faith community, time spent in Asheville and Washington, D.C., moving to Texas to be closer to my family, my friendship with you—the list goes on and on. None of this would have happened if my ex and I had stayed together. I wanted to write him a letter and thank him for divorcing me—or better yet, write a county-western song about it."

As I looked back over my list, I was filled with such gratitude to have put this behind me, but I was equally grateful for all that I had learned in the process.

Consider This: List no more than six guideposts that will mark that you've moved on.

48

Life Anew: From Broken Heart to Open Heart

Over the course of my breakup and while writing this book, I spoke with many people. Without exception, all of them agreed with this statement: no matter how difficult this time is for you, it will pass. Eventually, you'll move on and begin life anew. The quality of your life moving forward will be determined in large part by how well you've processed the pain, learned your lessons, and set intentions.

When Christopher and I broke up and I began this journey, my only thought was to stop the pain. I never dreamed the final destination would be my divinity. **I learned that if I can be present to whatever is happening in my life—even something as awful as a breakup—then I could also be present to the Divine. And the more I'm connected with the Divine, the more I'm connected to my essence and to pure love.**

Like attracts like; it's a universal law. In a state of divine connection, we are more likely to attract a partner who is a soul mate. I know this for a fact because three years after my breakup with Christopher, I met the man who would become my life partner. (Read about my journey in my book, *In Search of The One: How to Attract the Relationship You've Longed For.*)

Call me a romantic, but I believe we are wired to be in relationship. We are programmed to love. There's something within each of us that seeks to love and be loved. We long to be seen, heard, and understood—to have another human being bear witness to our lives. Yes, we will get hurt. Our hearts will break, and if we are lucky they will break open. When they do, we can begin to experience ourselves, relationships—indeed all of life—in a deeper, richer, and more meaningful way.

49

Lessons Learned About Moving On

- Clean house. Return, throw out, or pack away all reminders of the relationship, including framed photographs, gifts, and souvenirs. Delete cell phone listings. Take a look at your friends, diet, activities, and habits and decide if there's anything you'd like to change.

- Holidays can be particularly challenging. Consider creating a new tradition, shaking it up, or doing something for someone else. If worse comes to worse, remember it's only twenty-four hours.

- Set an intention. Draft an ideal relationship profile. See my example in chapter forty-five.

- It is possible to remain friends with your ex, especially if you were friends before you became romantic. Also it's important to take a break after your split.

- Delay dating until you are ready. Pay attention to your emotions and motivations around dating. If you do date, notice if you're comparing your date to your ex. Above all, don't date until you feel really good about yourself.

- Be patient with the process. Expect two steps forward and one back. Remember, you are still moving forward, and hopefully you're moving forward consciously.

- Remember that your ideal partner is the person who can lead you back to a more authentic relationship with yourself and the Divine.

- You will love again. The quality of your next relationship will be determined in large part by the work you do now. Be present to the pain, take time for introspection, and set your intentions. At that point, you'll be in the perfect position to attract the partner you've always longed for.

May I Ask You a Favor?

Thank you for sharing my journey. I hope you found it helpful in yours. If you did, may I ask you a favor? Would you help me spread the word? Please write a favorable review on Amazon and Goodreads and recommend this book to others who are experiencing a breakup.

I've enjoyed spending this time with you. Let's stay connected on Facebook and on my websites: LinkToRandy.com and RandySiegelWrites.com.

Appendices: Toolbox

I've compiled several lists and resources into a toolbox that may be particularly helpful to you as you break up, wake up, and move on. They are:

- Seven Commandments for Conscious Parting
- Ten Tools for Letting Go, Learning the Lessons, and Moving On
- From Breakup to Breakthrough: Twelve Questions to Ask Yourself
- Additional Resources

Seven Commandments for Conscious Parting

We've covered a great deal of information. If you don't remember anything else, I hope you'll remember these seven guideposts for conscious parting:

1. **Allow.** Allow all feelings and thoughts to bubble up. Don't try to control, speed up, or manipulate the process. Everyone's process is different. Allow yours to naturally unfold.

2. **Observe.** Observe your feelings, thoughts, and actions without judgment. Become an "observer-participant" in your life. When you are an observer-participant, you experience your emotions, but you don't identify with them. For example, you may say, "I *feel* sad," rather than "I *am* sad."

3. **Feel.** Feel your emotions. Remember that the more you're able to tolerate the pain, the more present you'll become, and the more present you become, the more you're able to tolerate the pain. If you don't experience the pain now, it will most likely creep back into your life later.

4. **Review.** Review past relationships. The twelve questions in these appendices should be helpful. The answers will help you grow and be more intentional as you move forward.

5. **Remember.** Above all, remember to be present. To be present is to wake up. When you catch yourself dwelling on the past or what may happen in the future, gently come back to the present. You'll know you are fully present when you feel you're in the presence of the Divine.

6. **Act.** Act intentionally. What changes do you need to make in order to bring your dreams, values, and interests in closer alignment with your relationships and life? Before acting, ask yourself if you are acting out of fear or love.

7. **Become.** Become your best self and live your best life. Allow, observe, feel, review, remember, and act intentionally. Your breakup will eventually become a breakthrough. You'll become the person you were born to be, and you'll enjoy richer, deeper, and more meaningful relationships.

Ten Tools for Letting Go, Learning the Lessons, and Moving On

Tool 1. Ask for No Contact

At first, it's a good idea to agree to no contact. In time, a friendship may develop. No contact creates closure and will help you let go, learn the lessons, and move on.

No contact means no contact. No meetings, phone calls, e-mails, texts, Facebook posts, or messages in a bottle. For any reason. Also, ask friends not to share any news about your ex-partner—at least for a while.

Tool 2. Clean House

Make space for something or someone new to come into your life. Return all your ex-partner's stuff. Leave his or her closet and bedside table drawer empty. Pack up any reminders, including photographs and letters, and put them out of sight. Delete old e-mails and telephone listings. Finally, assess your friends, your diet, habits, and activities, and choose the ones you want to continue and those you'd like to let go.

Tool 3. Practice Presence

This is often a tough order, but make every effort to stay in the present. Your mind will likely wander off into fantasy or other forms of "crazy thinking," but try to simple observe the emotions underlying those thoughts instead of trying to control or crush them. With practice, the act of observation serves as a kind of restart button to become present. When you catch yourself in a fantasy or other forms of "crazy thinking," ask yourself this question: "What's so bad about the present moment that I cannot be in it?"

Through this process, I learned that sensations are a clear pathway to the present. When I listen for the sounds around me, see my surroundings with what the Zen Buddhists call a "beginner's mind," and follow sensations in my body to track what I am feeling, I sink deeper into what Eckhart Tolle calls, "the power of now."

Tool 4. Consider Ritual

"Ritual is the art of giving visibility to invisible intentions," explains Laura Collins, a good friend, former Presbyterian minister, and an expert on rituals. Laura has a business called Living Rituals that performs a wide variety of rituals, from weddings to what she calls "sacred separations." Rituals—such as clearing the house after Christopher left—helped me prepare my psyche to wake up and move on.

Tool 5. Journal

A relationship expert once wrote that a journal is like a clean, sterile gauze pad for a seeping wound. Journaling is a simple and effective tool that can help you develop a greater understanding of who you are, how you came to be the way you are, and what direction you should take. It's also a safe place to release the multitude of thoughts and feelings bubbling up inside you. Record your thoughts using a variety of tools: write letters, make lists, and create dialogs between you and your ex—or between you and an aspect of yourself that needs an outlet (such as Sad Self or Higher Self).

When you journal, write freely. Don't worry about spelling or grammar, and don't fuss over smudged ink or cross-outs. Your journal is for you and you alone. You may share it with someone later, but when you are writing, write for yourself.

Tool 6. Pay Attention to Your Dreams

You can learn a lot from your dreams. Carl Jung said that dreams are "letters from the unconscious." Keep pen and paper or a tape recorder by your bed, and get into a regular habit of recording your dreams. Some of the breakthroughs I experienced were first foretold in my dreams. Also, be patient; it can take up to six months for the conscious mind to catch up with the subconscious mind.

Tool 7. Consider Therapy

There are times in our lives when we need a little outside perspective, whether from a therapist or coach. My therapist was instrumental in helping me go from breakup to breakthrough. Ask friends for recommendations, but above all find someone you click with, someone you feel comfortable sharing it all with.

Tool 8. Don't Discount a Little "Woo-Woo"

I found that a little "woo-woo" from time to time was helpful. During those periods that I needed hope or direction, I sought help from various sources of divination. Visit any metaphysical bookstore and you'll find a plethora of divination tools. My favorites are Runes and the Osho Zen Tarot deck. Ask friends to recommend a good psychic, or ask your local metaphysical bookstore for a referral.

Tool 9. Get In Your Body

One of the best ways to become present is to get in touch with your body. I've experimented with a number of body-centered activities to help me pay attention to sensation and shift from the cerebral to the physical. My favorites are exercise, dance, massage, yoga, Pilates, and acupuncture. Experiment and choose activities that work best for you.

Tool 10. Draft Your Ideal Relationship Profile

Review the lessons you've learned in this and past relationships. From them, catalog your top "preferences." Keep it simple. Limit your list to twelve.

From Breakup to Breakthrough: Twelve Questions to Ask Yourself

1. Why did I attract my ex into my life? (We tend to attract or be drawn to people that reflect how we feel about ourselves, our lives, love, and relationships.)

2. Why was he/she the right person at the time?

3. What worked well in the relationship and what didn't?

4. What would I do differently next time?

5. How was this relationship similar to past relationships? Am I following a pattern? And if so, is this a pattern I want to continue or break?

6. What limiting beliefs were activated during the relationship? How about after the relationship? What activated them?

7. What was it I wanted most from my partner that I didn't receive or get enough of? Was it something I could have provided myself?

8. What was I most proud of in our relationship? What brought me the most shame?

9. What new habits did I develop in the relationship? Do I want to keep them or let them go?

10. What disowned traits did I project on my ex-partner? (We tend to be attracted to people who have traits that we also possess but have disowned. For example, I've always been attracted to gentle men.)

11. How did I exit the relationship? In what ways did I avoid time and intimacy with my partner? (Some might include watching television, playing computer games, or reading novels.)

12. Was there a central lesson in the relationship? How about the breakup? If so, what were they?

Additional Resources

Books

Almaas, A. H. *The Unfolding Now: Realizing Your True Nature Through the Practice of Presence*. Boston: Shambhala, 2008.

Bach, Tara, PhD. *Radical Acceptance: Embracing Your Life with the Heart of a Buddha*. New York: Bantam, 2003.

Baggett, Leland. *Waking Up Together: An Interactive Practice for Couples*. Asheville, NC: R. Brent and Company, 2009.

Beattie, Melody. *Codependent No More: How to Stop Controlling Others and Start Caring About Yourself*. Center City, MN: Hazelden, 1987.

_____. *The Language of Letting Go*. New York: Hazelden, 1990.

Blum, Ralph H. *The Book of Runes: A Handbook for the Use of an Ancient Oracle: The Viking Runes with Stones*. New York: St. Martin's Press, 1998.

Bridgers, William, PhD. *Transitions: Making Sense of Life's Changes*. Reading, MA: Addison-Wesley Publishing Company, 1980.

Chapman, Gary. *The Five Love Languages: The Secret to Love That Lasts*. Chicago: Northfield Publishing, 1992.

Chodron, Pema. *When Things Fall Apart: Heart Advice for Difficult Times*. Boston, MA: Shambhala Publications, Inc., 1997.

Cope, Stephen. *Yoga and the Quest for the True Self*. New York: Bantam, 2000.

Cushnir, Raphael. *The One Thing Holding You Back: Unleashing the Power of Emotional Connection*. New York: Harper-Collins, 2008.

DeAngelis, Barbara, PhD. *How to Make Love All the Time*. New York: Dell Publishing, 1987.

Dispenza, Joseph. *God on Your Own: Finding a Spiritual Path Outside Religion*. San Francisco, CA: Jossey-Bass, 2006.

Hendrix, Harville, PhD. *Getting the Love You Want: A Guide for Couples.* New York: Harper & Row, Publishers, Inc., 1988.

Hudson, Russ, and Don Richard Riso. *The Wisdom of the Enneagram: The Complete Guide to Psychological and Spiritual Growth for the Nine Personality Types.* New York: Bantam Books, 1990.

Johnson, Robert A. *Inner Work: Using Dreams and Active Imagination for Personal Growth.* San Francisco: Harper, 1986.

Kasl, Charlotte. *If the Buddha Dated: A Handbook for Finding Love on a Spiritual Path.* New York: Penguin Group, 1999.

_____. *If the Buddha Married: Creating Enduring Relationships on a Spiritual Path.* New York: Penguin Group, 2001.

Kingma, Daphne Rose. *Loving Yourself: Four Steps to a Happier You.* Boston, MA: Conari Press, 2004.

Kübler-Ross, Elisabeth, and David Kessler. *On Grief and Grieving: Finding the Meaning of Grief Through the Five Stages of Loss.* New York: Scribner, 2005.

Lesser, Elizabeth. *Broken Open: How Difficult Times Can Help Us Grow.* New York: Villard Books, 2004.

McClary, Cheryl, PhD. *The Commitment Chronicles: The Power of Staying Together.* Naperville, IL: Sourcebooks, Inc., 2006.

Osho. *Osho Zen Tarot: The Transcendental Game of Zen* (cards). New York: St. Martin's Press, 1995.

Thesenda, Susan. *The Undefended Self: Living the Pathwork of Spiritual Wholeness.* Madison, VA: Pathwork Press, 1994.

Tolle, Eckhart. *A New Earth: Awakening to Your Life's Purpose.* New York: Plume, 2005.

_____. *The Power of Now: A Guide to Spiritual Enlightenment.* Novato, CA: New World Library, 1999.

Williams, Margery. *The Velveteen Rabbit: Or How Toys Become Real.* New York: Doubleday, 1922.

Other Resources

The Blueprint of We: getstarted.blue   The Blueprint of We is a conscious contract between two people in relationship. It outlines personal preferences and expectations, and provides a plan of action if you decide to break up.

Enneagram: enneagraminstitute.com   The Enneagram is one of my favorite models for human psychology and spirituality. While there are many excellent sites on the subject, I especially like this one.

5Rhythms   5Rhythms is a movement meditation practice created by Gabrielle Roth. Roth teaches that by moving the body, releasing the heart, and freeing the mind, one can connect to the essence of the soul. The five rhythms are: flowing, staccato, chaos, lyrical, and stillness. They are danced in sequence, known as a "Wave." I found this practice a wonderful way to work out emotion. Google to see if there's a group close to you.

Sacred Separations: sacredseparations.com   On this site, my friend Laura Collins, a spiritual counselor, offers a self-guided workbook for people wanting to review and release past relationships and create a vision for future relationships through exercises and ritual.

YourInternalGPS.com   If you would like to work with me individually, contact me through YourInternalGPS.com or RandySiegelWrites.com. Please note: I take a limited number of clients each month.

About Randy Siegel

Randy Siegel believes that love and work give us the greatest potential for growth because that's where our inner challenges are most visible. Since 1998, Siegel has inspired thousands of professions worldwide to "stand in their power by becoming the full expression of all they are" for such organization as the Recording Academy (The Grammy Awards), State Farm Insurance, and the American Alliance of Museums.

Siegel has written four books and currently is writing a fifth on how to find the relationship you've always longed for. He's written articles for *Balance Magazine*, the *Washington Post*, and other publications and is frequently quoted by the media. Siegel, his partner, Don, and their dog, Loodle the Poodle, divide their time between Asheville, North Carolina and Saint Simons Island, Georgia.

Connect with Randy through Facebook or his websites LinkToRandy. com and RandySiegelWrites.com. He'd love to stay in touch.

Other Books

In Search of The One: How to Attract the Relationship You've Longed For
The Inspired Life: How Connection and Contribution Create Power,
    Passion, and Joy
Engineer Your Career: Package, Present, and Promote Yourself for Success
PowerHouse Presenting: Become the Communicator You Were Born to Be

All are available through Amazon.com.

Workshops

Randy teaches occasional workshops on intimate relationships as a spiritual path. If you or your group is interested in hosting Randy, please contact him at Randy@RandySiegelWrites.com.

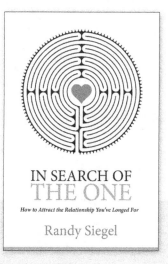

CPSIA information can be obtained
at www.ICGtesting.com
Printed in the USA
LVHW080224030919
629748LV00014B/682/P